ARTHUR LEE

Merry Christmas!

Arthur Lee

Alone Again Or

BARNEY HOSKYNS

4

CANONGATE

Originally published in hardback in the UK and simultaneously
in North America in 2001 by MOJO Books, an imprint of
Canongate Books, 14 High Street, Edinburgh EH1 1TE

This edition published in 2002

10 9 8 7 6 5 4 3 2 1

British Library Cataloguing-in-Publication Data
A catalogue record for this book is available on request
from the British Library

ISBN 1 84195 315 6

Typeset by Patty Rennie Production, Glenbervie
Printed and bound by Grafos, Spain

www.canongate.net

For Arthurly

Contents

Acknowledgements

THE AUTHOR WOULD LIKE TO THANK THE following: Arthur Lee, the late Bryan MacLean, Jim Irvin, Pat Gilbert, Jamie Byng, Harvey Kubernik, David Kamp, Sara Scribner, Don Waller, David Housden (at The Castle fanzine, Big Sky Studio, Stonecross House, Fitton End Road, Gorefield, Wisbech, Cambridgeshire, PE13 4NQ), Ben Edmonds, Steve Powell, Kevin Delaney, John Head, Eugene Manzi, Jac Holzman, David Anderle, Pamela Des Barres, Rodney Bingenheimer, Kim Fowley, Harold Bronson, Dan Epstein, Robert Leslie Dean and Paul Body.

Prologue
Hollywood Confidential

HIGH UP IN LAUREL CANYON, WITH ALL OF Los Angeles spread out around him, Arthur Lee sits and stares and contemplates death – "sitting on a hillside, watching all the people die", as he sings it in The Red Telephone, the brilliantly creepy song that concludes the first side of Love's *Forever Changes*.

"The Red Telephone was real, man," he will say 25 years later. "It wasn't The Twist or The Mashed Potato."

It is 1967, and all the world is caught up in the joy of flowers and beads and drugs, swimming in the colours that swirl through the psychedelic haze. Down on Sunset Strip, where for a year Love reigned as the hippest band in town, hippie kids float about in a state of cosmic bliss. But Arthur Lee wants no part of it. He's either seen too much or not seen enough; no-one is too sure which.

"I don't think Arthur wanted to leave his space," Bryan MacLean, the singer and rhythm guitarist who provided the vital foil to Lee in the original Love line-up, later reflected. "I think he was even mildly agoraphobic. Every place he lived, he'd have gates to his house. He liked to hang out and hold court behind those gates. He liked to have guys around him from his old neighbourhood that looked up to him and respected him – his courtiers. He would venture out to score whatever he needed, whether chemical or sexual, and that was it. He didn't hang out, he didn't show up at clubs."

"Arthur was so difficult to get along with," remembers David Anderle, in those days the chief A&R scout at Love's label, Elektra Records. "I spent so much time with him just talking, but there were other times when he would just become this other sort of guy. He was always afraid of something, and I could never figure out what it was. He was *such* an enigma. He didn't hang out on the scene like a David Crosby, he was more like a Brian

Wilson or a Captain Beefheart. That's how I think of him, really, as one of the LA greats: Brian, Beefheart, Zappa, Neil Young, Arthur . . . all haunted, reclusive, baffling people."

"Arthur was, and perhaps still is, one of the smartest, most intelligent and finest musicians I ever met in my entire career of making records," says Jac Holzman, founder of Elektra and now president of Discovery Records. "As large as his talent, however, was his penchant for isolation and not doing what was necessary to bring his music to his audience. His isolation cost him a career. Which was a shame, because he was one of the few geniuses I have met – in all of rock'n'rolldom."

It is July 1993, and I am sitting opposite Arthur Lee in a restaurant on Van Nuys Boulevard, on the other side of Laurel Canyon from Hollywood. Thirty years ago, Arthur could probably have looked down on this very spot from his gated eyrie atop Lookout Mountain. Now he lives here in the Valley with the mere mortals.

It's clear that Arthur is already a little tipsy, and he will down three or four more Bloody Marys during the course of our conversation – if "conversation" describes a rambling interchange in which he dodges, and for the most part evades, the point of my questions. He informs me that after many years of vegetarianism he's started eating meat again, because he was "getting too passive". He is still lean and handsome, it must be said, though still fond of a cheap and unsubtle hairpiece. (Thirty years ago, the rumour goes, Lee nodded out on heroin after applying a particularly corrosive brand of hair straightener to his barnet. Hours later he awoke to find it had all but destroyed the follicles on his scalp.) He is also still possessed of considerable charm.

"I went on a big campaign for a year, telling everyone not to drink," Arthur grins at me. "But, well, you know . . ." His voice trails off into an indistinct sigh. The word is that Arthur did actually achieve sobriety for the aforesaid year, and was even engaged to a girl he'd met through Alcoholics Anonymous. Whether this is the same girl to whose nearby apartment he later takes me, I choose not to ask. The girlfriend in question seems fairly together if faintly exasperated by Arthur, who all but ignores her as he busies himself with making me a tape of

Rosa Lee Brooks's My Diary, a cracking little soul single he produced way back in 1964, and which features (so he claims) the very first session ever played by his friend Jimi Hendrix.

A story about Hendrix, as it happens, is one of several disjointed anecdotes with which Arthur regales me in the restaurant in Van Nuys. In 1969, it seems, Jimi and Arthur were holed up in San Diego together, and Hendrix brought a call girl up to Arthur's hotel room as a present for his friend. According to Arthur, the guitarist then joined them in bed, but – get this – proceeded to come on to Arthur rather than to the girl. When I evince eye-bulging disbelief at this claim, Arthur gives me a nervous laugh, then protests that "I'm *serious*, man!"

Unsure exactly what to believe, I suspect there is a subtext at work here, and one that has much to do with Arthur's bitterness at the way Hendrix, Sly Stone and others appropriated his black rock/psychedelic soul style and then received all the kudos for it.

"He was a friend, that's how I like to think of him," Lee once said of Hendrix. "He was also the greatest guitarist I ever saw in my life. But you gotta remember I was into all that freaky underground thing before he came along – I remember when he came out, with the hair and clothes and everything. It made a great impression, but I'd been doing those things for a long time, wearing 40 pounds of beads, two coats, three shirts, and wearing two pairs of shoes on one foot and glasses with one lens one colour and one the other, ha ha!"

"I was the first black person wearing those clothes and doing that stuff," he reiterates to me. "And then the credit went to Jimi." Oh, the pain of being a forgotten pop pioneer – the one who never sold any records.

"We constantly referred to the fact that Arthur was black and I was white," Bryan MacLean is telling me, "but it was in an ironic way. I'm sure it crossed my mind that this was kinda cool – that this could work to our advantage – but we never thought we were gonna change the world."

I am sitting beside MacLean in an open-topped red pick-up, flying down Sunset Boulevard with a hot wind on my face. It is August 1996, almost three years after my encounter with Arthur Lee.

MacLean is a total surprise. I'd expected some fey,

fragile, born-again Brian Jones, and what I get is a burly surfer guy, a little like Gary Busey at the end of John Milius's Big Wednesday: big and intense and just slightly crazed, talking 19 to the dozen as he bombs along Sunset towards the Pacific Ocean. This is a man, it transpires, who runs 2½ miles up to the Griffith Park Observatory at dawn each morning from his Los Feliz apartment, then runs back down again. "I get to the top when the sun comes up, and that's when I pray," he says. "The coyotes used to run with me, but I haven't seen them lately." So much for the Beverly Hills pretty boy who, at the age of 18, sang Softly To Me in an artless folk-pop tenor.

Much of what Bryan MacLean says on a long drive that takes us all the way down to Venice and back is shot through with anger towards Arthur, albeit anger tempered by awe at the man's talent and the spell he seemed to cast over everybody during that heady 1965–67 period. Thirty years later, when it's too late to stand up to him, Bryan rages at the way he allowed Lee to push him around.

"Arthur had the dominant personality, so his songs got done," he says matter-of-factly. "I was writing prolifically all through those years, but when we went into the studio he'd say no to every song. If I was lucky I'd get one or two. Had I been tougher – *physically* tougher – I'd have grabbed him by the collar and thrown him up against the wall."

"There was a slightly twisted, almost homoerotic relationship between Lee and MacLean," says David Anderle, a tall, wryly amused man who's worked closely with more than his fair share of pop eccentrics. (He even attempted to run The Beach Boys' Brother label for a year.) "Let's just say Arthur made Bryan's life miserable. I always had the feeling that Arthur's personality was so dominant that Bryan felt he couldn't do much unless the hole was made for him to speak or move."

The Lee-MacLean relationship – or dichotomy, or dialectic – would survive three extraordinary albums: *Love, Da Capo* and the majestic *Forever Changes*. These records were among the best that Los Angeles had to offer in the '60s, and they were all about the yin and the yang of beauty and anger, grace and psychosis.

After MacLean quit the group and moved into a twilight zone of fear and religious rebirth, Lee soldiered haphazardly on into the ensuing decades as a maverick black rocker. In 1996, after a quarter-century of rumour and mishap, he was arrested and charged with discharging a dangerous weapon in a public place. A convicted felon, he pleaded not guilty and wound up being sentenced to 12 years in jail.

Alone again, naturally ...

The Love story is one of the stranger and more compelling narratives of '60s and '70s rock'n'roll: a tale of dread and dysfunction, creative miscegenation and unrealised greatness. At the centre of it all is Arthur Lee himself, a black freak in a white world, a perversely self-sabotaging sage, an enigma perhaps even to himself.

Was Arthur one of the all-time rock greats or was he just an opportunist who happened to seize a moment of pop incandescence? Was he, in the words of David Anderle, someone "with a bigger vision than just making dumb rock music", or did he just cannily exploit the spirit of Sunset Strip? Was he a genius or a rogue?

What if he was both?

1 Summer's Children

WHEN ARTHUR LEE AND BRYAN MACLEAN first met in the summer of 1965 – in the parking lot at Ben Frank's coffee shop, then the epicentre of all that was moving and shaking on Sunset Strip – Love had already been going for several months. Except that they weren't called Love, they were called The Grass Roots, and they had evolved out of two bands (The LAGs and The American Four) that Lee had led before seeing the folk-rock light at an early Byrds show.

Lee had been born not in Los Angeles but in Memphis, on March 7, 1945. The name on his birth certificate was Arthur Porter Taylor (his father was a trumpeter named Chester Taylor), but he took the surname of his stepfather Clinton Lee after his parents divorced and his mother Agnes remarried.

"My mother was very light-skinned, she could pass for white," he told me. "She was a schoolteacher, and she came from a long line of schoolteachers." Memphis played little part in Lee's musical education, even if The LAGs were styled after Booker T. And The MG's, but he claims he remembers his early childhood there "very clearly" and that his aunt "used to play Muddy Waters and Howlin' Wolf every morning".

Uprooted and brought to California at the age of five, Lee, in his own words, was "an only lonely child" whose sole solace seemed to lie in music. "I started giving him music lessons when he was about 10 or 11," Agnes Lee recalled on the phone from Memphis, to which she had returned from LA recently. "His teacher told me that he could play better than she could, and that he didn't need to take any more lessons." What was Arthur like as a child? "He was a spoiled brat (*laughs*), but he had a good heart."

Lee grew up in the Crenshaw-Adams district of Los Angeles, where his stepfather worked as a builder and decorator. "When I was a little boy I would listen to Nat 'King' Cole, and I'd look at that purple Capitol Records logo," Lee said. "I wanted to be on Capitol, that was my goal. Later on, I used to walk from Dorsey High School all the way up to the Capitol building in Hollywood [a journey of several miles] – did that many times. I was determined to get a record deal with Capitol, and I did, without the help of a fancy manager or anyone else. I talked to Adam Ross and Jack Levy at Ardmore-Beechwood, I talked to Kim Fowley, and then I talked to Capitol."

Unfortunately, The LAGs' sole Capitol 45 rpm release, the sub-Booker T./Jimmy Smith instrumental Rumble-Still-Skins, was a woeful disappointment when it appeared in 1963, reflecting poorly on the teenager's talent. "It was terrible, really a disgrace," admitted Arthur, who claims he "didn't trust anybody" and therefore didn't play Capitol his best songs.

"I wasn't singing then; I didn't sing until the Love band," he told Zigzag's Giovanni Dadomo in 1974. "The record didn't do anything. I was young and very inexperienced and I was testing the record company. I figured if I gave them my worst stuff and they ripped me off I wouldn't get hurt. But it didn't work, so after that I started giving my best, and I've been doing that ever since."

Lee never graduated from Dorsey High, where he'd excelled at sports. "I played basketball there and had the school record for most points in a single game, but at 6'1" I was too short." He says he was too busy plotting his musical career. ("I wanted to be the best pop artist in the world, that was my ambition.") While at high school he watched the R&B singer Johnny "Guitar" Watson step out of a gold Cadillac wearing a gold suit and flashing gold teeth, and "knew then that I had to have a guitar".

In fact, the lure of gold might have led him into another lifestyle entirely. According to Bryan MacLean, Lee was "known as the baddest guy on the West Side of LA, the Cassius Clay of the streets". The singer's street name, said MacLean, was "Polo": "All his friends would be, like, 'Yo, whassup, Pol?' He had a rep, man. He was the man in his neighbourhood." (In point of fact, MacLean may have confused "Pol" with "Po": Agnes Lee says Arthur was nicknamed "Po" as an abbreviation of his middle name, Porter.)

Lee's first real musical accomplice – and a man who would stick with him right through to *Forever Changes* – was guitarist Johnny Echols, who'd lived next door to jazz legend Ornette Coleman on 27th Street and learned to play guitar with Adolphi Jacobs of The Coasters. When Lee formed The LAGs to play R&B covers at local parties, Echols was his first recruit. And when The LAGs turned into The American Four and recorded Luci Baines for Bob Keane's Del-Fi label, Johnny Echols – like Lee a light-skinned black kid with processed hair – was still there at his side. (Arthur says he and Echols were very influenced by the look of Bobby Womack and The Valentinos, who had "long hair and stuff I'd never seen in my life". He claims he even went to see J.W. Alexander, who ran Sam Cooke's SAR label, to which The Valentinos were signed. J.W. wasn't interested.) Luci Baines was essentially a revamp of Twist And Shout, with Arthur doing a decent impersonation of Manfred Mann's Paul Jones; the song's eponymous heroine was modelled on Lyndon Baines Johnson's dance-crazy daughter.

For Bob Keane, Lee not only recorded as the leader of The American Four but produced soul and Chicanopop singles for Li'l Ray (a Spectoresque version of Ben E. King's I Who Have Nothing) and Ronnie And The Pomona Casuals (the disposable dance-fad songs Slow Jerk and Everybody Jerk). "I never made a penny from Bob Keane," he claimed, though an American Federation of Musicians contract for Luci Baines shows that he may actually have netted the princely sum of $61. (The track can be found on the 1994 Del-Fi compilation *Sun, Surf, Cars And Guitars*.)

For the ultra-obscure Revis label, Lee wrote and produced the aforementioned My Diary, hiring recently-fired Little Richard sideman James Marshall Hendrix to play on it after seeing him back The O'Jays at the California Club on Western and Santa Barbara – a venue where The American Four were enjoying a brief stint as house band.* For Lee, Hendrix's sound was "sort of like, well, you take Curtis Mayfield and his riffs, and turn your amps up full blast, and you see what you get".

The left turn into white pop came partly as a result

* Eva Records of France released an album called *Black Beauty* in 1997, collecting all Lee's pre-Love releases and productions, including tracks by The American Four, Ronnie And The Pomona Casuals, Li'l Ray and Rosa Lee Brooks.

of seeing The Beatles on The Ed Sullivan Show – "I was sitting there on 27th Street and they knocked me out . . . I knew that I had to do that too" – and partly because Lee got wind of a happening new scene up in Hollywood in the early spring of 1965. The Byrds were playing at Ciro's on the Strip, and Lee and Echols went to check them out. Lee was blown away by the new freedom of Beatles-influenced folk-rock, and by the chiming sound of Jim McGuinn's 12-string guitar.

"The whole scene was great, man," he remembered later. "I took advantage of a trip that was going down that I saw. [The Byrds] kind of opened my head to the direction I went on my first album. Because . . . there weren't too many long-haired musicians then, The Byrds were about the first I'd seen. In Hollywood, anyway. The Beatles and the Stones, they were out. But from Hollywood or my home town, I didn't see very many long-haired groups. So I saw a thing, and I flashed on myself when I saw them. They were doing a trip I knew I could do, man."

As much of a revelation was seeing Mick Jagger singing Time Is On My Side on The Red Skelton Show, and catching The Rising Sons – the short-lived, blues-based band formed by Taj Mahal and Ry Cooder – at the Ash Grove on Melrose Avenue. "That's when I really knew something was happening," he said (though he hastens to add that "we were the first integrated rock band, because The Rising Sons weren't a rock band").

Lee even had a close encounter with a Rolling Stone at Ciro's. "Brian Jones got kicked out because he didn't have any ID, which you had to have to get an alcoholic beverage," he told John Tobler. "Brian was coming this way, and I was going that way. I looked at him as weird as he looked at me, you know. I never met any of The Rolling Stones – I don't care to. But I do look in the mirror occasionally, and I do see a Rolling Stone."

"Arthur was playing R&B," said Bryan MacLean, "and somewhere along the line he decided to take a ride up to the Strip. I don't think it was opportunistic. I don't think he thought, 'Oh, I wanna get in on this.' I think he sincerely liked the music and the scene." A name change from The American Four to the trendier-sounding Grass Roots was in itself almost enough to earn the band – Lee, Echols, drummer Don Conka, and bassist John Fleckenstein – a gig at the Brave New World on Melrose.

"I named the group The Grass Roots behind a trip, or an album I heard that Malcolm X did, where he said, 'The grass roots of the people are out in the street doing something about their problems instead of sitting around talking about it.'"

Barely a month after seeing The Byrds, Lee gave his band a comprehensive makeover, junking the previously obligatory covers of Shotgun and Louie Louie and embracing the punkier, more British Invasion-style sound that would be heard on Love's debut album. It was as though McGuinn and friends had somehow formed a sonic alliance with Messrs. Jagger and Richard.

Bryan MacLean, meanwhile, had grown up in an environment very different from the one which spawned Arthur Lee. He was a golden child of privilege, a kid whose parents mingled with Hollywood celebrities. "I can remember being at my dad's house, up in Benedict Canyon," he told David Fricke. "He had a living room with a side that was all glass, overlooking the city. I used to put his classical records on. I could see my reflection in the sliding glass doors, in the glass walls. And I would dance at night over the lights of the city."

MacLean's first sweetheart was a pubescent Liza Minnelli. "She and I would do songs from The Wizard Of Oz," he told me. "She'd be at the piano. My whole background was Rodgers and Hammerstein – as a kid I'd stand in front of the mirror and conduct. I'd put on stage make-up and costume and stand in front of a full-length mirror. I created my own world." The composer Frederick Loewe, of My Fair Lady fame, was a neighbour and declared the boy a prodigy at the age of three.

MacLean says the idea of performing was "just a fantasy" at this stage, and that his real aim was to be a painter. But one day he swung by the Sandal Shop in Westwood – one of the sales outlets for his paintings – and heard a group of people singing Appalachian ballads. The conversion to folk music and its culture was instant. Soon he too was singing and playing guitar in coffee houses and clubs like the Balladeer and the Troubadour. On other occasions he'd listen to a young Ry(land) Cooder at McCabe's Guitar Shop. When I met Bryan in 1996, he still remembered the night he first heard David Crosby perform Hey Joe.

It was through befriending Crosby that MacLean,

in the early summer of 1965, came to be hired as a roadie by The Byrds. "For a 17-year-old kid it was heaven," he all but cackled as his pick-up careened down Pacific Coast Highway. "Crosby and I got along perfectly. I didn't understand what everybody was complaining about, because he was just like me!" (Read: a belligerent brat.)

But The Byrds wore Bryan out. "We did 30 one-nighters," he remembered. "I was so exhausted I started to hallucinate. When I began to screw up, The Byrds went to England and didn't take me with them. I got back to LA and The Byrds were gone. The upshot of this was that the little bands were vying for the spot as the kings of LA."

MacLean parted company with The Byrds shortly before their English tour in August '65, "and when I came back to LA there was a whole scene that The Byrds had created, but without them". MacLean says he knew nothing about Arthur Lee prior to meeting him at Ben Frank's. He even claims Lee looked "so strange and unusual that at first sight I couldn't determine his gender". When the two got talking, Lee told MacLean about The Grass Roots and MacLean hipped Lee to his relationship with The Byrds. "He invited me to come and hear him at the Brave New World," said Bryan, "and for some reason he ended up in my car. He needed to get somewhere and I said I'd drive him. And that was the beginning of it."

MacLean said that the band he saw was "a black version of folk-rock". He told Lee he'd cut off his arm to join. Lee acceded to MacLean's wishes, but only after a few gigs with another serious contender: future Manson Family murderer Bobby Beausoleil, who would go on to form his own band, The Chamber Orkustra, up in San Francisco (and, later still, compose the music for Kenneth Anger's infamous Lucifer Rising). "He was known as 'Bummer Bob'," recalled Arthur. "I never had anything to do with him other than auditioning him. People told me Manson used to come to my shows. I never knew that."

Beausoleil remembered seeing The Grass Roots support The Byrds, and he was desperate to join a band. "One day I went to Arthur Lee and I told him I thought he needed a rhythm guitar player in the band," he remembered. "They were getting ready to play a gig at a place called the Brave New World. It was a gay bar, although they didn't know it at the time – or at least I didn't. But it was a gig that Arthur didn't expect to be attended that well, so he decided I could get on stage with them. Arthur saw the potential in having some pretty white guy in the band, apart from the musical potential.

"The first couple of nights we played there, it was all gay people. After I played a few sets over a few evenings, I went up on the Strip one night on our break. I just got tired of the situation – we were all tired of it, we wanted an audience. So I went out on Sunset Strip and told everybody: this is where it's happening, and I gave out directions to the Brave New World. By the time I got back to the club, people were already starting to arrive, and between that set and the next, the place was packed."

Bobby Beausoleil was in The Grass Roots when the Watts race riots erupted in south-central LA in August 1965 – riots which must have seemed particularly pertinent to a "two-tone" band like the Roots. "We actually went into Watts, because Arthur wanted to check on his mom," recalled Beausoleil. "We all drove down into there, and it was really strange. There were military vehicles, police out everywhere."

"Bummer Bob" maintained that when he took a quick trip up to San Francisco, Lee brought in MacLean.

"I went back down to LA and found out that I'd been replaced in the band, and the reason was that I was too young to play in many of the clubs legally." MacLean, he said, took advantage of his absence. Even so, Beausoleil made his mark: according to him, the band's name change was directly inspired by his own nickname, Cupid.

"Just before I went back to San Francisco I was at Ben Frank's on the Strip, where the colourful people used to go for coffee and cake and hang out. I was there by myself, getting ready to leave, and ... Arthur came in and sat down with me. He told me that he'd decided to re-name the band Love in honour of me, alluding to the Cupid nickname that I had. I felt honoured. It kind of healed the hurt feelings."

"Arthur was smart to get me in the band," MacLean told me, pointedly not referring to Beausoleil. "I think he let me join more for who I knew than for what I could do. I brought him the whole Byrds scene, first at the Brave New World and ultimately at the Whisky A GoGo. And we became the king of the street bands in Hollywood."

Rodney ("Mayor of Sunset Strip") Bingenheimer

recalls that Love were one of the first bands he saw after moving down to LA from northern California. "He was this black guy, but he always seemed like part of the white scene. He wasn't playing soul, he was playing this jangly guitar music. It was almost like he was like the black Roger McGuinn." (Bingenheimer, incidentally, has maintained contact with Lee ever since, and accompanied him to London in 1994 when Alan McGee invited them both to Creation Records' 10th anniversary bash at the Albert Hall.) In the fall of 1965, Lee was obliged to surrender the name The Grass Roots to the identically-named combo on Lou Adler's Dunhill label, who hit the charts with Let's Live For Today and a version of Bob Dylan's Ballad of A Thin Man.

"We were The Grass Roots of Los Angeles," Lee told John Tobler in 1974, "and a Grass Roots band from San Diego came down when Barry McGuire was opening a club called the Trip on Sunset Strip. And, I don't know, man, they took our name. I didn't have it recorded that we were the original Grass Roots, so they took the name . . . instead of going to court and fighting it and crying and all that shit, I thought I'd just call the group Love . . ." In fact, the name had been registered by Dunhill staff writers/ producers P.F. Sloan and Steve Barri. (MacLean initially suggested the name Summer's Children as a replacement: it had been the planned moniker for a band – another interracial band, interestingly – he'd almost started with Taj Mahal.)

Lee didn't make the same mistake with the name Love. "I went down and registered it legally," he said. "Everybody is Love, that's the way I feel about it. I'm part of everybody, everybody's Love. It's a great name." None of his musical henchmen was too enthused about it, however.

Around the time of the name change, the band found its first managers, Jerry Hopkins and Doug Lyon. ("In view of their unreliability and general hard-to-get-along-with attitudes," Hopkins remembered, "I suggested they instead call themselves Fist, but they didn't think that was at all amusing.") The duo came to see them during their new residency at a fairly nondescript little joint on North Ivar Street called Bido Lito's.

"The club was pretty small," Hopkins said in 1973, by which time he was a leading rock writer with Rolling

Stone and other magazines. "On entering . . . you went through a small courtyard and entered by a jukebox, with the bar straight ahead of you. As you made a sort of U-turn there was this small dance floor with a few odd tables and chairs around it, and at the far end a little stage. And there, Love played pretty much nightly." Hopkins said that if there was a big enough audience, the band members would get $5 each for the gig. If (as often in the week) there wasn't, then the owner would cancel the show. Thanks to Love, Bido Lito's became "one of the true underground clubs in LA".

Central to this transformation was a troupe of freaks led by Sunset Strip scenester Vito Paulekas, the son of a Lithuanian sausage maker who'd settled in Massachusetts. Vito, said Jerry Hopkins, was "a short, wiry guy . . . a craggy-faced dude who was very much on the scene" and who "loved to dance, loved to have a good time, loved to throw or sponsor dances and was a scene-maker in the true underground sense".

Vito had established himself at Ciro's, and – in Hopkins's words – "so identified with the early Byrds that [he and his crowd] accompanied the band on their first tour". According to Hopkins, the entourage then moved to Bido Lito's and became Love fanatics: "[Vito] wanted to go on and launch Love like he'd helped to launch The Byrds." It was no coincidence that Bryan MacLean was living in an apartment above the Paulekas pad in Hollywood. "It was Vito, Carl Franzoni, Sue, Beatle Bob, Bryan and me," Lee told me. "Bryan put a ribbon in his hair, and people would come to Ben Frank's to hang out with us after we played shows."

When Hopkins and Lyon offered to manage the band, Lee agreed, but with these provisos: i) they had to sign to a big company, ii) he wanted a billboard on Sunset Strip and iii) he wouldn't play any clubs on the Strip unless Love had top billing. "You see, he was totally convinced he was going to be as big as Jagger," said Hopkins. (Arthur compromised on all three counts, as it happens: they didn't sign to a big label, they didn't get their billboard, and they played second on the bill to The Turtles at the Trip.)

Hopkins managed to persuade his contacts in the music business to come and see Love at Bido Lito's. Artie Kornfeld came down, as did David Anderle, then with MGM. "The troubles started almost immediately," Hopkins told Zigzag. "Every time a record company executive came down, someone in the band wouldn't show up . . . We were getting nowhere fast; all we were doing was running out of record companies, who were getting fed up having their time wasted by unknown groups who didn't even turn up to play."

Finally, Hopkins and Lyon opted to record Love themselves and booked time in the late fall of 1965 at the Original Sound studio on Sunset. At 3am – and $350 lighter of pocket – Love and their managers emerged with five tracks, including versions of My Little Red Book and Hey Joe. "It was take after take until poor Arthur was hoarse and crawling to the control room for a little encouragement before he went back and had another try," remembered Hopkins. "We weren't very happy with the results – none of us; it was a painful session for all concerned." Everyone was feeling their way in the dark, with no studio experience and an engineer who "wanted to go to bed". Lyon took the tape around Hollywood's A&R men and was politely laughed out of their offices.

*

It is hard now to imagine what a dash Love must have cut when they first broke through on the Strip at the tail end of 1965. On one level they were one of a number of LA bands walking a thin line between folk-rock and garage-punk. But on another they were unique: a "two-tone" band playing an amazing hybrid of folk, soul and psychedelic pop at a time when there were still strong racial and stylistic divides in the American music industry.

At the centre of it all was Arthur, a black freak on the white scene, a ghetto punk in beads and pebble glasses. "Arthur was the first guy who really had that LA look, with the fringe jacket and the Levi's and the little glasses," said David Anderle. LA luminary and spoken-word producer Harvey Kubernik recalled that he and his friends "got our whole wardrobe" from Lee and Love: "We all went to Sy Devore Devoss in Hollywood and bought those big belts and whale cords."

"In 1967, every kid with a dollar in his pocket was walking around with chandelier crystal glasses," said Jerry Hopkins. "But Arthur had had a pair in 1965, which was really far out. To complicate matters further, one lens was blue and the other red. God only knows how he walked in them, but he was always wearing them. I hear that he used to drive in them too! Bryan used to wear a cape, but I suspect he got that idea off David Crosby."

Lee was initially ribbed by old friends, but the teasing didn't last long. "After the guys in my old neighbourhood saw my success, they slapped me on the back and bought wigs and chequered pants and triangular glasses." Robert Rozelle, bassist in Love's '70s line-up, remembered the first time he met Lee at Bido Lito's: "My goodness, I'd never seen anything like him before: he was a freak. Then they started playing and I'd never heard anything like that in my life."

"Lee cut quite an imposing figure," wrote Three Dog Night's Jimmy Greenspoon in his autobiography One Is The Loneliest Number. "Dark glasses, a scarf around his neck, Edwardian shirts and – what was to become his trademark – an old pair of army boots with one unlaced. He had a mesmerising presence . . . The audience became followers of King Arthur Lee. He was a Pied Piper who would lead them down the road to a different form of consciousness."

"I can remember feeling edgy years ago watching

Lee emerge, spectre-like, from the dark of the parking lot across the street from Bido Lito's, his guitar strung across his shoulder like a weapon," wrote Stuart Goldman in the Los Angeles Times many years later. "Like Clint Eastwood he projected an aura of danger. On-stage, he was totally captivating, twisting and turning through the songs like a man possessed. He played splashing guitar and riveting harmonica and he'd tread the apron of the stage, always looking as if he was about to fall off. He seemed to court disaster."

When Lee snarled his venom-fuelled version of My Little Red Book – a Burt Bacharach and Hal David song that Manfred Mann had recorded for the soundtrack of What's New Pussycat? – it was clear that Los Angeles had found its very own Mick Jagger. Only this one was a black Mick Jagger, a guy that LA music-biz veteran Denny Bruce describes wittily as "a black American imitating a white Englishman imitating a black American".

"My Little Red Book I put in because I'd seen the movie What's New Pussycat? and liked the way Paul Jones did it," Lee later recalled. "I just added a bit of hard rock and that was that."

At this point Lee confined himself mainly to singing and playing harp, though he would periodically don a twin-necked Gibson for visual effect. Playing lead on most of the band's songs was Johnny Echols. "[Johnny] told me I couldn't play guitar because my left hand wasn't active," Lee remembered. "It took me about a year to learn how to press the string down for a note to sustain." To Lenny Kaye, Lee said, "I played My Flash On You and a couple of other really easy, simple trips just to change the stage appearance of the trip. I really wasn't a guitar player. Bryan played guitar and Johnny played guitar."

The British influence was only too manifest in Lee originals like Can't Explain, its title borrowed from The Who and its drum fill from the Stones' Get Off My Cloud. But the mesh of guitars – Lee's, Echols's, and MacLean's – was pure LA, as were the Byrdsy You'll Be Following and the mournful pangs of Message To Pretty and Signed D.C., the latter a stark first-person account of drummer Don Conka's heroin addiction. (Message To Pretty, like My Diary before it, was about Lee's "first love" Anita, whose parents didn't want her consorting with such an obvious bad apple.)

From the outset a highlight of Love's live set was MacLean's frantic rendering of Hey Joe, delivered without a vocal safety net at every show. Like Louie Louie, it was one of the primal punk songs. "Bryan really was the first to popularise Hey Joe in the LA clubs," says Robert Leslie Dean, a Love fanatic from the band's inception, and years later a member of The Bryan MacLean Band. "Bryan had learned the tune from David Crosby while he was The Byrds' road manager, but The Byrds did not come out with their version until a few months later."

"The way Crosby had done it, it almost had a Mose Allison type feel," MacLean remembered. "When we did it, it was like punk rock. I lost my voice every night singing it. It was completely new – folk rock with a punk edge – and it put us on the map." Ironically, neither Love nor The Byrds would have hits with the song: that honour was reserved for a cash-in band called The Leaves – and subsequently, of course, for Jimi Hendrix.

"The Leaves glommed on to the tune after coming down to Bido Lito's," says Robert Leslie Dean. "Backstage after one of the sets they asked the band how the song went, and Johnny or Bryan wrote down the lyrics for them."

"From what I can gather," said Jerry Hopkins, "a couple of guys from The Leaves . . . asked Bryan for the lyrics. Bryan, being the surly, moody type, refused, but Arthur, with somewhat uncharacteristic benevolence, said, 'Oh go on, give 'em the words.' So Bryan laboriously wrote them out, but refused to tell them who'd written the song. The Leaves subsequently released the song as a single and authorship was noted as 'Traditional/Public Domain.' But it bombed and they went back in the studio and re-recorded it." This time, produced by Nik Venet, it was a hit.

Love may have missed out on the action with Hey Joe, but the record deal they sought was just around the corner.

2 The Castle

IT TOOK MACLEAN'S LIVE VERSION OF HEY JOE
at Bido Lito's to convince a 34-year-old New York record
executive that he'd "found the band I was looking for".

Jac Holzman's Elektra label had been a bastion of
folk music on the East Coast, but Holzman could see the
times they were a-changin' and – like Atlantic's Ahmet
Ertegun with The Buffalo Springfield, whom Holzman
had originally wanted to sign – made up his mind to
muscle in on the emerging West Coast action. "I was
getting antsy about finding a breakthrough act for
Elektra," he recalled in Follow The Music, his oral history
of the label. "I had no Lovin' Spoonful, and New York was

being picked over by record business players with lots of pop experience."

Holzman was urged to see Love by Ronnie Haran, an ultrahip chick who worked at the Whisky A GoGo and would soon be playing a part in the rise of The Doors. In his book, Holzman describes the scene at Bido Lito's the first time he saw Love play: "It was a scene from one of the amiable rings of Dante's Inferno. Bodies crushing into each other, silken-clad girls with ironed blonde hair moving the kind of shapes you didn't see in New York, to a cadence part musical and all sexual."

Love were already on-stage when Holzman arrived. "The band was cranking out Hey Joe and My Little Red Book," he wrote. "Inwardly, I smiled. My Little Red Book was by Burt Bacharach and Hal David, and featured in the Woody Allen movie What's New Pussycat? Hip but straight. And here were Arthur Lee and Love going at it with manic intensity. Five guys of all colours: black, white and psychedelic . . . my heart skipped a beat."

After the show, Holzman offered the band a deal. With folk music manager Herbie Cohen serving as an intermediary, Lee demanded a $5000 advance, got it and the next day blew $4500 of it on a gold Mercedes 300 gull-wing. The rest of the advance went on a new harmonica, with the other members receiving a measly $100 apiece.

"[Arthur] was this kind of brooding, dark presence," comments Mark Abramson, Holzman's second-in-command, in Follow The Music. "He wore these jewelled glasses that he obviously couldn't see through, low on his nose. He always looked at you over them, so he had this look of a kind of berserk intellectual or teacher or a judge or a guru of some sort. He would sit back and talk, and it would make a lot of sense until you tried to figure out what he was actually saying."

By late January 1966 the band, complete with new rhythm section Ken Forssi (bass) and Alban "Snoopy" Pfisterer (drums), were cutting their first Elektra album at the Sunset Sound Recorders studio. "Snoopy was a groupie that was in the audience," Lee recalled. "He came up to me and said he played drums, and anybody that could carry a back beat was about all I was using at the present, because Don Conka, I couldn't get the cat together, man."

"They really knocked me right out," Snoopy told

MOJO. "The power and drive and energy and funkiness . . . [it was] beyond anything I'd ever heard." (Snoopy was still at college, which is why he's the only one with short hair on the album cover.)

Love was recorded at the Sunset Sound studio between January 24 and 27, 1966, and produced by Holzman with Mark Abramson. Engineering was a "new kid" called Bruce Botnick, who thought the band were on acid for much of the time. (Lee, he notes in Follow The Music, was "so high all the time that he wasn't high . . . he had achieved what they call clear light".)

"Arthur frequently played someone else's instrument if he thought he could play it better, and he always could," noted Holzman. "Once, we had completed a take using up all four of our available tracks. Arthur still wanted to add a harmonising vocal on track three. With no tracks available, I asked him if he was sure he could get it on the first take. He stared at me over his glasses as if I was some sort of alien bug."

The results were engaging if primitive. "What you hear on that first album is just an enervated, attenuated version of what we were like live," Bryan MacLean told me. "It didn't have the distortion or the energy or the impact." Maybe not, but *Love* remains one of the better debuts of its time, a punky, pumped-up mix of rockers and ballads. "When their first album came out, I just fell on the floor," said Jerry Hopkins. "I couldn't believe it was the same band. It was then that I realised the importance of someone who knows how to work in the studio, to advise and direct a group and to get the best out of them."

My Little Red Book, which ascended to the giddy height of Number 52 on the US singles chart, sizzled, as did Hey Joe and the unashamedly similar My Flash On You. ("Don't force your smuggled drugs my way," Lee sang on the latter, "'Cos I cleansed my soul and that's how it's going to stay!") Gazing was like an acid-age remake of The Crystals' Then He Kissed Me – LA teen symphonics mutating into jangled psychedelia. Lee later admitted that Johnny Echols had all but written Emotions, an instrumental track used on the soundtrack to Haskell Wexler's 1968 counter-culture classic Medium Cool. The gentle, ethereal Mushroom Clouds – with lines like "little children dying in an age of hate" – leaned closer to fey Simon & Garfunkel folk-pop, while the jazzy Latin chords of

MacLean's Softly To Me presaged his superior Orange Skies and Alone Again Or.

Lee's clever, acerbic lyrics on *Love* reflected the seismic changes in post-Dylan songwriting. "Dylan was the breaking point," Arthur admitted. "I remember seeing The Byrds, and they were doing Dylan and I thought, That's me, and I thought I could do it as well, if not better, so that's when I switched from R&B to writing catchy lyrics and hot licks."

With its cover portrait (stamped with Bill Harvey's custom-made "Love" logo) depicting the band as a gang of hip Sunset Strip hoods, *Love* trumpeted the presence of a major new musical force on the LA scene*. The picture was shot in the grounds of Bela Lugosi's old estate in Laurel Canyon.

By the end of the year, Love's influence would be felt strongly in the sound of bands like The Seeds, The Leaves, The Lollipop Shoppe and The Music Machine (whose Talk Talk was pure Love). Sixpence (later The Strawberry Alarm Clock) covered My Flash On You on

* In July 1974, Lee asked Giovanni Dadomo if he'd ever noticed how on Love's album covers Elektra "used to do everybody the same colour . . . it cracked me up, man . . ."

the flipside of their Fortune Teller, and The Sons Of Adam recorded Lee's off-the-cuff psych-punk classic Feathered Fish. (According to Ken Brooks in Arthur Lee: Love Story, there was "great animosity" between Lee and The Sons Of Adam's Randy Holden, later of Blue Cheer. Feathered Fish was apparently about Arthur's girlfriend of the time.)

By the time the record was released in May 1966 (with the catalogue number 74001, indicating the start of a new series for Elektra), Love were the toast of the town's underground, playing sold-out residencies at Bido Lito's and at the Hullabaloo on Hollywood Boulevard. "We were the biggest group in LA," Arthur said. "The street where Bido Lito's was, that whole street from Selma Avenue to Hollywood Boulevard, was packed with people. At the Hullabaloo we had people lined up all the way down to Sunset."

Bryan MacLean remembered these days as ones of innocent mischief. "We were just having a ball," he said. "We didn't care about the implications of being a multi-racial group or about civil rights. There was just as much of a racial gag going on between Arthur and Johnny as between Arthur and me or Johnny and me. We'd be riding around, holding, and Johnny would say it looked suspicious – a white guy in a car with 'a spade and an Ethiopian'! I liked Arthur's music and I liked the way he got my sense of humour. A lot of what people thought was snottiness and cockiness was really self-parody. I was making fun of *myself*, the Beverly Hills brat who was suddenly on the hip scene."

For many of the budding girls on the Sunset Strip, MacLean quickly took on the status of pop pin-up. To Pamela Des Barres, self-proclaimed "teenage nymphet", the beautiful Bryan was "a golden, freckle-faced strawberry blond, the most delectable prize in Hollywood, most coveted and treasured by little dolls like myself". MacLean, she wrote, "completely epitomised the '60s Hollywood rock prince". After "spending a sunny day frolicking around at a Love-in in the presence of Love's most precious boy", Pamela was even moved to write a winsome little poem about him:

> *Carries a white dove*
> *Upon his shoulder*
> *If anyone doubts the peace within*

He plucks from the bird a feather
That erases doubts of war.

On his finger
He wears a ring of honesty
If this is doubted
He gives the ring away
And another appears in its place.

He carries a rolled rainbow
In his hand
If anyone doubts his love
He wraps the colours
Around their hearts
So all they can see is light.

It wasn't all "rolled rainbows", of course. Love were early masters of surly pop attitude, as reporters from teen magazines like KRLA Beat and Hit Parader soon learned: far from epitomising "the whole hippie thing", the band came on like the Sex Pistols a decade before their time. When KRLA Beat's Rochelle Reed interviewed them in June 1966 in the legendary "Castle" – the exotic mansion they were renting in the Los Feliz hills – they treated her abominably, psyching her out with mind games and telling her they'd met during a gang fight.

"Only when a group really reaches the top," Reed concluded school-marmishly in her story, "can their careers withstand what they may suffer from being continually rude and uncaring to fans and reporters alike. In my opinion, Love will soon be on many blacklists in the music industry, rather than in the 'little red book' where they want so badly to belong."

"I agreed with every word the girl wrote," MacLean told me as he drove up the winding street that led to The Castle. (It stands there to this day, now painted a burnt orange and doubtless owned by some sinfully rich movie agent.*) "We were just atrocious to her. But I didn't mean any harm. We were creating a persona – the bad boys of rock'n'roll! Kids who are neglected by their fathers go after negative attention, you know!"

* "The Castle" had already served as a very swanky *pied-à-terre* for all manner of visiting pop celebrities, including Bob Dylan and the Velvet Underground. It was where many of Love's promo shots were taken. One particular picture, taken on a stairwell – featured on the cover of Rhino's *Love Story* anthology – remains perhaps the best-known image of the band.

"I don't know, it was like we were all pretty young when we did our first album," recalled Lee in 1970. "Some of the cats in the group were really young in the mind, I found . . . I think maybe they were thinking about doing this trip and if it was accepted, then they could be the way they want or they could sort of have more balls, you know? They kind of got headstrong, after the first album . . . And I saw all that coming down, and myself even. So we changed, because we thought we were in this fantasy trip, we thought we had to make it, be Number 1, gold records. I'm not interested in that trip, really. I don't care, I'm just trying to do my own thing and tell these people what I see."

But any fears that such arrogance was premature were allayed that month when Love cut the mind-shattering 7 And 7 Is at Sunset Sound Recorders. "It was about Anita, my high-school sweetheart," said Arthur. "The relationship lasted a year, although she was going out with someone else the whole time. I was trying to prove myself to this girl and her parents because I didn't have a college degree or nothing."

Lee later surmised that he "might have started punk

rock" with 7 And 7 Is, and he may be right. To say that it is one of the great rock singles of the '60s would be a sorry understatement: it's an apocalyptic masterpiece, hurtling furiously along for two and a quarter minutes like some unholy Roky Erickson fusion of Hey Joe and Peggy Sue before climaxing in the sound of an atomic bomb:

> *When I was a boy I thought about the times I'd be a man*
> *I'd sit inside a bottle and pretend I was in a can*
> *In my lonely room I'd sit, my mind in an ice cream cone*
> *You can throw me if you wanna 'cos I'm a bone and I go*
> *Oop-ip-ip, oop-ip-ip, yeah!*

It required over 30 takes to get the Herculean drum track for the song, with Lee and Snoopy switching back and forth under the anxious eyes of Jac Holzman and Bruce Botnick. "I know that I had to stand there, stand in front of Snoopy and coach him," Lee told John Tobler in May 1974. "I had to do that with that first group all the time." No-one seems to recall definitively who actually played on the take that made *Da Capo*, but it's generally accepted that Lee took over from Snoopy after take 30.

Blasting away any folk-rock preconceptions lingering from Love's debut, 7 And 7 Is spelled out the obvious, which was that the band had plunged head-first into the oceanic realm of hallucinogenic drugs:

If I don't stop crying, it's because I have got no eyes,
My bible's in the fireplace and my dog lies hypnotised!

Or:

Through a crack of light I was able to find my way
Trapped inside a night but I'm a day and I go
Oop-ip-ip, oop-ip-ip, yeah!

The single became Love's biggest hit, reaching Number 33 in America and paving the way for the group's second album. (No. 14, the song's eventual B-side, was recorded as a joke, according to Lee.)

On September 27, 1966, the band went back into the studio – back to a new beginning with *Da Capo*. In the producer's seat this time was Paul Rothchild, whose work on the Paul Butterfield Blues Band's epic and influential

East-West had so impressed Lee that he too wanted to include an extended blues-based track on the album. Bruce Botnick engineered with Dave Hassinger assisting.

Before the session, Lee informed Holzman that he wanted to renegotiate terms of contract, based on the fact that he'd signed to Elektra while still a minor. In the new contract, the royalty rate was upped to seven per cent. "To look at Arthur," noted Holzman in Follow The Music, "it would never occur to anyone that he was a minor. He was a heavy ingester of substances and he wasn't Dorian Gray. I didn't know Arthur's age, and Al Schlesinger, the attorney who represented him and Love in the formal contract negotiations, didn't suspect either." With Schlesinger's help, "we worked out a resolution, increasing Love's royalty from five to seven per cent, plus other reasonable adjustments."

Da Capo, recorded in September and October 1966 at the RCA-Victor studio in Hollywood (where the Stones had cut Satisfaction), was a giant step forward from Love, introducing a psychedelic and almost baroque edge to the band's garage-folk sound. Snoopy had moved to harp-sichord by this point, with former Sons Of Adam member Michael Stuart taking over on drums and Tjay Cantrelli joining the line-up on flute. ("Everything I ever played in Love," Snoopy recalled, "was either written down, because I'd had eight years of classical training and could read music OK, or it was explained to me exactly by Arthur – and that went for both keyboard and drums.")

"I figured that with the [second] album, instead of a folk-rock trip, I'd just do what's in me, you know?" Lee told Lenny Kaye in 1970. "I feel that I found myself, or planted a seed of who I am today, in the *Da Capo* album."

The only thing *Da Capo* had going against it was the side-long epic Revelation, Love's very own Goin' Home (the long blues track on the Stones' *Aftermath* album). Although he "almost cried when I heard Goin' Home . . . because I'd been doing that trip two years before that came out", Lee later slagged off the track as "the lousiest effort we ever did".

"I never understood the idea behind Revelation," said Bryan MacLean. "I guess it was hip to do a whole side like that, but I had songs which would have carried on the style of the first side. I think Arthur was concerned that it would be discovered that I was a force – that it wasn't just him."

Had its second side "carried on the style of the first side", *Da Capo* would probably rank alongside *Forever Changes* as a Summer of Love classic. Certainly there are few more remarkable sequences of music than Stephanie Knows Who, Orange Skies, ¡Que Vida!, 7 And 7 Is, The Castle and She Comes In Colors, six sublime songs that blend psychedelia and punk rock with Latin and Broadway influences.

Stephanie Knows Who was about the girlfriend of one Israel Zacuto, a member of local band Wolfgang, while Orange Skies – like Softly To Me before it – stemmed from Roger McGuinn's guitar break on The Bells Of Rhymney. ¡Que Vida! was originally known as With Pictures And Words and (with Lee on drums and Snoopy on organ) took nine long hours to nail down. Although The Castle was putatively written for Lynn Johnson, a girl who couldn't decide between Lee and MacLean, Lee's passion for New Wave cinema (he was a big Godard fan and saw Fellini's Satyricon countless times) suggests the title may be a reference to the Franz Kafka novel. The song was later used in England as the theme music for the TV programme Holiday '71.

"*Da Capo* was the ultimate of what I call show-tune rock," MacLean told me. "See, what you have is a guy who grew up on Rodgers and Hammerstein and Aaron Copland, and who worshipped Burt Bacharach, and then a guy who grew up on R&B in the Crenshaw-Adams district. And it was that mixture that made it interesting and made it unique. The Love sound, if you want to be really honest, was Arthur copying *me*."

Self-serving as this sounds, it may not be so far-fetched when one considers the radical changes in Lee's writing on songs like ¡Que Vida! and Stephanie Knows Who – or, for that matter, the precipitous decline in the quality of his music after parting ways with MacLean. "Nobody else besides Bryan MacLean was writing music inspired by Broadway show music, with those kinds of melodies and chords and raised sevenths and augmented sixths," says Robert Leslie Dean. "Bryan was doing that."

"My theory is that Arthur didn't write all the songs he's credited with," says John Tobler, the self-styled Captain Of The Fleet In The Quest For Arthur Lee, whose early-to-mid-'70s Zigzag interviews with Lee (not to mention his Love *Masters* compilation of 1973) did much to keep the Love cult alive. "I think MacLean may have had quite a bit more to do with them than we realise."

The release in 1998 of MacLean's *ifyoubelievein* – for the most part a collection of lost solo tracks from the '60s – was intended to make this very point. A kind of missing link between balladeering David Crosby and early-Elektra period Tim Buckley, *ifyoubelievein* featured songs like Kathleen (about Bryan's mutt), the lovely Fresh Hope, and demo versions of Orange Skies and *Forever Changes*' Old Man and Alone Again Or. They were songs, MacLean noted, "written between the ages of 17 and 21, essentially on pure instinct, by a person who had neither musical nor lyrical training".

"I was away and my mother found a box of reel-to-reel tapes in my garage," he recalled on the album's sleevenotes. "I knew they were there, but not exactly what was on them. I wrote [those songs] a long time ago and many were never recorded. When she started shopping them, her motivation was this: that a certain amount of vindication needed to take place. Whenever you hear about Love, it's Arthur Lee and Love. My mother felt that people should know there were two people involved.

"I firmly believe that if things had been the other way around, by now you probably would've already heard a great deal, if not all, of what is assembled here. For one thing I would have stuck around the band a lot longer, not feeling the frustration of having a backlog of unpublished and unperformed material, and the natural unfulfilled desire for recognition or even vindication."

David Fricke perhaps overstates things in his sleevenote to the album when he writes that *ifyoubelievein* is "in a sense, the Love record that never was". But the songs bear out the suspicion that Lee took more than he acknowledged from MacLean's love of Broadway songs and flamenco. Lee, noted MacLean, "would always say, 'That's great!', but it would never end up on the record". The Orange Skies session of September 27, 1966 – with Lee commandeering the lead vocal – was almost the last straw. It was, said Bryan, "the closest Arthur and I ever got to a fist fight".

Love, says Bruce Botnick bluntly, "was Arthur, it wasn't a democracy". Adds Robert Leslie Dean: "Arthur *was* the leader. He was the guy with the strength and the intimidation, the fists if necessary, to make the final decision. Bryan was the second-in-command, he was the guy who'd work with Johnny and Kenny, but Arthur was the ringmaster. Bryan was the LA doll, the boy toy of the LA bands. And he was a hopeless romantic. He had gorgeous women around him, but he was a sensitive guy in his own way."

On the other hand, it was Lee who plucked My Little Red Book from the Bacharach and David songbook, Lee who worked the (subconscious?) quote from Jackie DeShannon's A Lifetime Of Loneliness into ¡Que Vida!, and Lee indeed who would go on to title *Forever Changes*' A House Is Not A Motel after Burt and Hal's A House Is Not A Home. MacLean may have written Orange Skies, but it was Lee who steered Love away from the pumped-up angst of Hey Joe towards a new strain of psychedelic muzak that David Anderle calls "punk with strings".

"Lee wanted to bring in very traditional folk elements; very light, almost white tones," Harvey Kubernik told the LA *New Times*. "But all that was first originated by black musicians. He brought it back around, but in a way he also brought American music forward, because he wasn't making dance music for your feet or body, he was making dance music for the mind. It was cerebral, musically and lyrically."

Underground rock gonzo Sandy Pearlman, a disciple of the legendary R. Meltzer, wrote that *Forever Changes* "finishes what *Da Capo* began – Arthur Lee's insane mutation of Mick Jagger into . . . Johnny Mathis!" "I did that on purpose," Lee told Giovanni Dadomo in 1974. "Right when I started, I decided I wanted to be a ventriloquist-type person, so when I'm told I sound a lot like Hendrix on one song, I'm glad, because that way there are no limitations. I really like mixing things like that. I'd love to hear Johnny Mathis do Foxy Lady, ha ha!, or Howlin' Wolf do Turn! Turn! Turn!"

"Love started out with a kind of garagey folk-rock, but once they got into their own style it wasn't like anybody else," says Bomp Records boss and psych-punk sage Greg Shaw. "It had a kind of orchestral sense to it which wasn't influenced by The Left Banke and didn't sound like Tim Buckley but which was really unique. Arthur could put together elements that you'd never think of putting together, and it would work."

"I want to put a nursery rhyme in your head and

tell you what I want you to hear with the nursery rhyme," Lee told Lenny Kaye. "What I love to do, man, is let them hum the nursery rhyme that I wrote and then take a trip and maybe work a change in their life . . . that's why I couldn't possibly be interested in the Top 40."

A key point about Love was how much closer they were to the LA pop tradition of Brian Wilson (and even The Association and The Mamas And The Papas) than they were to the loose live sound of the new San Francisco bands. As with such seminal LA psych-pop as Gene Clark's Changes, Lee leaned towards soft melody even as he sang of dark, difficult subjects. For The Grateful Dead or The Jefferson Airplane, it would have been anathema to use strings or flutes on a record. For Love, it was part and parcel of a Hollywood pop sensibility that led seamlessly to the lushly-orchestrated *Forever Changes*.

Tied in with this was Lee's distance from – or unwillingness to be part of – the new acid rock scene. "When we played up in San Francisco [Love made their Bay Area debut at the Avalon Ballroom on April 8, 1966, and played the Fillmore with the Dead, no less, on July 3], Arthur would just stay in his hotel room," remembers

Bryan. "I had a whole life up in San Francisco, but he didn't know *anybody* there. I think he was actually afraid of people." At the Fillmore West, concert overlord Bill Graham got into exactly the same kind of fight with Love that he'd had with those other classic anti-hippies The Velvet Underground. When Lee refused to go on-stage at the time Graham had stipulated, he found himself being dragged into the spotlights by the irate promoter.

Love were chronically handicapped by Lee's lack of interest in life outside Los Angeles. (The band didn't even play in New York till May 1968.) His obstinacy meant that the group spurned opportunity after opportunity that came their way: even their Elektra labelmate Jim Morrison was moved to comment that "I don't think [Love] were willing to travel and go through all the games and numbers that you have to."

"Arthur was always very aloof," says Harvey Kubernik, who saw Love in all their incarnations and later interviewed Lee in his capacity as West Coast correspondent for Melody Maker. "He didn't exactly lead the league in schmoozing, and he certainly never understood the concept of ingratiating yourself. See, even Neil Young knew how to work the room: he had some idea of how the world worked and how to get people to work for him. The whole loner thing with Neil was perceived as an artistic impulse, whereas with Arthur it was just about how difficult he was to work with. Arthur blocked people off from getting to know him. The whole point about those glasses he wore was that you couldn't see into him. So not only was he ornery and aloof, but he presented himself in terms of, 'Don't come too close.'"

"We didn't do the things we should've done," Lee admitted to Lenny Kaye in 1970. "We were always on the trip of wanting to do the right thing at the right time, making sure everything was the right time for us. And we passed up a lot of things, man. Like, I didn't particularly want to eat shit, you know? Coming out to New York with the offer we got to come with was like eating shit. That's what I thought at the time."

"The whole thing," he told John Tobler in 1974, "was really based around my so-called ego during those latter years of the '60s, because I just didn't feel like playing sometimes, you know. With The Grass Roots band, we had gigs playing in clubs and we got a few concert offers and what have you, and it was a pretty loose thing. I liked what I was doing, and I liked to keep it that way and then all of a sudden we became the Love group, and everybody expected to be under the Beatle bed or whatever [sic]... I mean, I need money just like everyone else, if everyone else ever needed money, but man, I'm not gonna eat shit on the road to become a so-called pop star."

Bryan MacLean put things more tersely: "We broke covenant with our record company by not co-operating, not making it worth their while to distribute our music. I didn't know any better – I really was naive as far as business was concerned – but I think Arthur did." (Liz McKee, Bryan MacLean's mother, informed me that Arthur was business-savvy enough to sign all the other members of Love to his own production company, which meant that all their royalties went directly to him. She claimed her son never received a penny in royalties from either Softly To Me or Orange Skies. John Tobler says that MacLean only started receiving royalties for Alone Again Or in the late '70s, after the song was covered by British hard-rockers UFO.)

To Snoopy Pfisterer, Arthur "tried to do everything

by himself, with no manager, nothing . . . he wanted top billing in everything – if it wasn't The Ed Sullivan Show, then he wouldn't do TV". *Da Capo* was, in any case, Snoopy's swansong. "In the first place, I didn't ever intend to be a professional musician," he told *Zigzag* some years later. "I couldn't play the drums worth a fuck when I joined Love, and I was even worse when I left . . . I mean, I got through that time with those fucking heavies – they were so fucking heavy with all their heavies that I got heavied out, man, and instead of improving over the two years I regressed . . . I mean, there were some really heavy scenes went down there, man."*

"Arthur was phenomenally talented, probably more talented than anybody in town, and he knew it," reflected Jac Holzman in Follow The Music. "He hungered for success, always reaching for the brass ring, but it would just pass him by. In his career and his rela-

* Post-Love, Snoopy moved from one group to another – apparently because of "my personality hang-up, man . . . I have problems getting along with people". He wound up in prison in Mexico in late 1969 and was then deported. He moved on to Costa Rica, where he'd lived the first 10 years of his life (his father was an architect for the American Foreign Service), and to Panama. Finally he washed up in Europe, where he even auditioned for T.Rex

tions with the company he was a basket case." He added, "Deep down, I have always believed that Arthur's refusal to travel was because he wanted to stay close to his connections."

Bryan MacLean's "one great desire throughout that period" was for "someone to come along and manage us – someone with a strong enough personality to take over the reins from Arthur . . . but it never happened". Perhaps the most self-sabotaging decision Lee made in Love's career was to turn down the invitation to play the Monterey Pop Festival in June 1967, conceivably on account of a grudge he bore against festival organiser Lou Adler (for robbing him of the name The Grass Roots?), though more likely because by then – when work was starting on *Forever Changes* – the band was already in a state of drug-crazed chaos.

For a long time there was a theory that Lee had taken umbrage at the supposed favouritism displayed by Elektra towards labelmates The Doors. (As late as 1993, Lee was grouching to the Los Angeles Times that "[Elektra] used the money they made off us to promote The Doors and make them Number 1".) The irony here is that it was

Lee who urged Jac Holzman to see The Doors playing at the Whisky, and who even persuaded the Elektra boss to check them out again after he – like many record executives in Hollywood at the time – was left unimpressed by Jim Morrison's heavy-handed stage act.

For their part, too, The Doors signed to Elektra primarily because of Love, whom they worshipped. "Jim Morrison used to sit outside my door when I lived in Laurel Canyon," says Arthur. "He wanted to hang out with me, but I didn't wanna hang out with *anybody*." (In Arthur Lee: Love Story, Ken Brooks claims that Lee stepped out with Pamela Courson before she began her romance with Morrison.)

"I'm sure Elektra would have provided backing for a promotional tour," said Jerry Hopkins in 1973. "Holzman was not only very anxious to get into rock but he really believed in Love, especially Arthur. Holzman's a good judge of talent and he saw Arthur for what he was. Arthur was difficult, hard to please, and he'd change his mind a lot. In later years he changed Love's personnel too much, I felt . . . maybe his head was too big. He certainly had a huge ego, which is alright if you can channel it properly but I don't think Arthur ever had the necessary self-discipline."

"When I came to Elektra, it was Love-land," says David Anderle. "Very quickly it became Doors-land. It had nothing to do with The Doors being all-white, it was just that the Doors thing was so *fast*. Nor was Arthur apparently that desperate for the success The Doors had. He was the night creature! As was Jim, of course, but . . . there was some big fear cloud with Arthur. Believe me, Holzman loved Arthur, but something happened to him, and I don't know if it was drugs, alcohol, or *something* biochemical."

"Arthur Lee was like a tiddlywink," remarked Holzman himself. "Just when you thought you had a grasp of what he was about, he would do something surprising and get out from under you."

"It's pretty obvious that they were eclipsed by The Doors," says Rhino's Harold Bronson, "It's not fair to say The Doors were better, but The Doors would do anything."

Drugs certainly played their part in Lee's seeming lack of ambition. After the release of *Da Capo*, the band's road manager, Neil Rappaport, introduced the group to heroin, which soon had Lee, MacLean, Echols and Forssi in its grip. "You kind of didn't care," says MacLean. "There was a little stigma attached to it – it was a little deeper in. Arthur was the one who turned me on to it, though I was what you'd call a chipper or weekender. Johnny and Kenny got real bad." (So bad, indeed, that in the early '70s the duo became known infamously as "The Doughnut Robbers" after a series of armed robberies of doughnut stands around LA. Both men did time for the robberies.)

In a bizarre twist to the tale, Rappaport, a long-term junkie, was later rumoured to be have been killed by the band (his drug-overdose death was commemorated in *Four Sail*'s Your Friend And Mine). However, this rumour probably has its origins in Snoopy Pfisterer's claim that Rappaport had died after Johnny Echols had prepared a hit for him.*

* Jac Holzman told Zigzag in 1973 that he'd recently run into Johnny Echols and had "asked him about all the rumours that he'd been found guilty of manslaughter, had murdered the roadie and been in jail. He said that was nonsense, and that several of the people had been in custody for an hour or so, while the police sorted it out, but then he'd been released immediately, and that the rumour had been sped on its way by another member of the group, who for the purposes of libel shall remain nameless."

Word of Love's heroin use spread quickly through the rock community, confirming their outsider status and making them *personae non gratae* at the big flower-power party during that Summer of Love. Many people found the band not just surly but intimidating, profoundly at odds with the prevailing spirit of peace and ... well, love. In San Francisco they were regarded with opprobrium: Greg Shaw's pioneering fanzine Mojo Navigator called them "a bunch of hoods", and Pete Albin of Big Brother And The Holding Company referred to them as Hate.

The issue of the name even bothered Bryan MacLean. "I remember lecturing all four guys in the band, the exact moment," he would tell Pamela Des Barres years later. "I was pacing back and forth on the oriental rug my dad had given me for my twenty-first birthday and saying, We have this name, how about trying to live up to it?"

"I don't want to say that Arthur was demonic," said David Anderle, "but he was very manipulative and destructive. See, Arthur was not really a hippie, he was more of a punk than a hippie. There was almost a gangster thing going on there – rule by intimidation. But at the same time, he could be so sweet. It was totally schizoid."

3 Bummer In The Summer

IF LOVE *WERE* HOODS, THEY WERE PSYCHEDELIC hoods: the tension between punk and flower power – between menace and beauty – lay at the heart of what made their music so compelling.

Nowhere was this more evident than on *Forever Changes*, the album the band began recording at Sunset Sound in June 1967, the very mid-Summer of Love, and finished at the end of September. As with more than a few classic albums (e.g. *Astral Weeks*, *Exile On Main Street*, *Electric Ladyland*), the circumstances of its creation hardly augured well.

First off, Neil Young, then still a member of The

Buffalo Springfield, was lined up to co-produce the record, but couldn't commit to anything more than helping to arrange The Daily Planet. "*Forever Changes* started out as a project that Neil Young and I were going to produce," remembered Bruce Botnick. "The Buffalo Springfield were a bit shaky and I thought Neil could use a new direction and perhaps play some guitar on the LP. When the time came to start, Neil was unable to fulfil his role because of his obligation to the Springfield. He was going through some changes and he wasn't physically well at the time. So he dropped out and it was me. Love were going through a terrible time. There were lots of personal problems and the band hadn't played live for a while."

"We used to work every night," Lee told Relix magazine in 1993, "but after we started making money, the more we made, the less we worked, the less we were a unit, and Love deteriorated. People's personal habits started to come before the music. Initially they would listen to me because I wrote 90 per cent of the songs. After we became successful, they got big heads, every-body had a house, a car, a flash Cadillac. They didn't need me. Money spoiled them – it spoiled me, too. It was a strange time. I thought I was gonna kick the bucket. But you still gotta keep on."

"The band was so untogether and playing so badly that I thought it would be a good idea to get in good rock studio musicians," remembered Botnick, who hired at least three veterans of Phil Spector's legendary "Wrecking Crew" – Hal Blaine, Don Randi and Billy Strange – for the opening session on June 9. "I was prepared to record the album with Arthur singing and playing on his songs and Bryan singing and playing on his songs, with backing by studio musicians. Arthur played the guitar and we worked out the guitar parts and arrangements there, and recorded two songs in three hours, The Daily Planet and Andmoreagain. The group were present, too. I remember [them] physically crying at this session. The band was so shocked, so put out, so hurt that it caused them to forget about their problems and become a band again. We kept the two tracks because they're good, but we did some overdubs to make it sound more like the band. It was a psychological ploy that worked."*

* The fact that Don Randi had played on Buffalo Springfield sessions prompts comparisons between *Forever Changes* and the

The presence of Blaine and co. literally shocked Love into action. Forssi remembered that it "scared all of us half to death".

"The band sat there and listened to the musicians recording Andmoreagain and The Daily Planet, and it sparked them," said Botnick. "They realised they'd blown it, got their act together, and recorded the rest of the album." When Love reconvened at Sunset Sound on August 11, there were no session musicians present. And by late September, when David Angel's horn and string parts were added, *Forever Changes* was finished.

Here, on one record, was the sound of Los Angeles undergoing a sea-change from jingle-jangle, Cuban-heel innocence into strange-days, Manson-era weirdness – the same direction in which The Doors were headed. If Lee

proto-"orch rock" of Neil Young's Broken Arrow and Expecting To Fly, as arranged by the late Jack Nitzsche. It's also possible that Wrecking Crew bassist Carol Kaye was booked to play on The Daily Planet and Andmoreagain: in a 1996 interview with DISCoveries, Ken Forssi remembered "this girl trying to get a bass part down and she couldn't do it because the song had so many changes". Forssi claims he offered to take over: "I said, 'Here, I'll do it . . .' [and] this happened with a couple of other songs, too, because they just didn't write the song and didn't know how it felt. You know, these people are used to reading charts, and you can't put some of the stuff we played on a chart."

could celebrate the Sunset Strip spirit of carnival on the exhilarating Maybe The People Would Be The Times, Or Between Clark And Hilldale (the latter pair being the cross streets that marked the start and end of the Strip's hippest block), on other tracks he took a far darker view of the hippie bacchanal. "I write about my environment," Arthur told Lenny Kaye. "That's what I constantly write about, what I see, what I think needs to be changed and what I think shouldn't."

"What I liked was the deep thought and soulfulness of Arthur's lyrics," says Robert Leslie Dean. "The cryptic imagery really fascinated me. Plus vocally, no one could touch Arthur Lee – no one in The Byrds, The Buffalo Springfield, The Doors, and all the northern Californian bands. Arthur Lee was and is a one-of-a-kind vocalist. Arthur was not just a soul shaker, he could sing blues, he could sing folk, he could sing pop."

Despite a musical palette more heavily weighted towards strings and mariachi-style brass than towards acid-rock guitars, the album had a fix on the surreal and disturbing flavour of the times that only The Doors (and perhaps the Brian Wilson of the lost *Smile*) matched. The effect was tantamount to oxymoronic, offsetting disturbing lyrics against pretty, almost Zombies-style melodies and coupling Arthur's pure tenor tones with the darkness of his subject matter. Particularly sinister were A House Is Not A Motel, Live And Let Live, and The Red Telephone.

"He described things that were very menacing," says writer/producer Harvey Kubernik. "We're coming out of the Summer of Love, and he's singing Bummer In The Summer. He's talking about racial tensions, tensions between men and women."

"You're just a thought that someone, somewhere, somehow feels you should be here," Lee sang on A House Is Not A Motel; "And it's so for real to touch, to feel, to smell, to know where you are here ..." Or try this for size:

> *By the time that I'm through singing,*
> *The bells from the school of war will be ringing.*
> *More confusions, blood transfusions,*
> *The news today will be the movies for tomorrow.*

> *And the water's turned to blood,*
> *And if you don't think so, go turn on your tub.*

And if it's mixed with mud, you'll see it turn to grey,
And you can call my name, I hear you calling my name . . .

Live And Let Live, meanwhile, was about the hypocrisy of condemning a man for shooting a bluebird while driving native Indians from their lands and caging its immigrants in ghettos: "I served my time, served it well," Lee sang bitterly. "You made my soul . . . a cell." (More startling still was the song's opening line, "Oh, the snot has caked against my pants." "I passed out, slobbered on my pants and woke up," Lee told Phil Gallo matter-of-factly. "It had crystallised. I wrote about it.")

The Red Telephone was the darkest statement of all. "Sitting on a hillside, watching all the people die," Lee began; "I'll feel much better on the other side." Nothing too equivocal there. And then: "I believe in magic, Why?/Because it is so quick/I don't need power when I'm hypnotised/Look in my eyes . . ." As the song builds through its second section, the protagonist seems to be floating in a kind of drugged *ennui*: "Life goes on here day after day/I don't know if I'm living or if I'm supposed to be/. . . I've been here once, I've been here twice/I don't know if it's the thirds, the fourths or the fifths to fix." By the end, though, the scenario almost recalls One Flew Over The Cuckoo's Nest: "They're locking them up today, they're throwing away the key/I wonder who it'll be tomorrow, you or me." As the track winds down we hear the famous phrase, "We're all normal and we want our freedom", taken from Peter Brook's Marat/Sade. Lee had seen the play six times.

"Arthur had this big house right on top of Mulholland Drive," recalled Ken Forssi, "and we'd look down over the city from there. Arthur would sit up there staring out and wondering about all the ambulances."

"By *Forever Changes*, when I did that album, I thought I was going to die at that particular time, so those were my last words. I was 26*. I'd always had this thing about when I was going to die, man, or physically deteriorate, and I thought it would be about 26 . . . something like that. I just had a funny feeling." In 1991, Lee told Goldmine's Frank Beeson that there was an "eeriness" about the album: "*Forever Changes* was to be my last words

* If Arthur's given birth date was correct and he was under 21 when he signed the Elektra contract, he couldn't possibly have been 26.

to this life. And it's like death is in there, so it's definitely forever changes." ("For the time that I've been given's such a little while," he sang on You Set The Scene; "And the things that I must do consist of more than style . . .")

The album is strewn with images of horror and mutilation – of guns and blood and sirens and accidents, of things that don't necessarily make much sense but stick stubbornly in the mind once heard: the "water mixed with blood" in A House Is Not A Motel, the toys which "plastic Nancy" buys to keep her kids "in practice/waiting on the war" in The Daily Planet, and of course the encrusted snot. On few other '60s albums does the Vietnam War hover so ominously in the background. Only Maybe The People Would Be The Times and Bryan MacLean's brace of songs (the sweepingly lovely Alone Again Or and the faintly sentimental Old Man) provide any kind of respite from the mood of spooky despair.

"You have to understand that Arthur's lyrics and music were all stream-of-consciousness," said Bryan. "I worked on my songs, I *constructed* them, but he didn't write that way. 'The snot has caked against my pants' came out . . . and stayed! [Laughs] He had a brilliant mind, but his biggest problem was trying to be hip. He was too hip for words. He talked like a 1940s jazz musician."

"Stream-of-consciousness" it might have been, but *Forever Changes* sounded anything but off-the-cuff. With its intricately crafted arrangements, idiosyncratic time changes, and overlapping vocal tracks, it fully merits its reputation as LA's very own *Sgt. Pepper*. Thirty years on from its release, however, there is still bitter argument as to who was or wasn't responsible for what on *Forever Changes*. At different times, Lee has claimed that Bruce Botnick did not co-produce the record, and that he himself wanted David Angel's strings removed from it.

"I, like, added something, an orchestra or something behind my trip to see what kind of feeling I could get out of that," he told Lenny Kaye. "So that's just my trip . . . they are all pieces to be used, the way I look at it. Musicians are merely arrangements." To me he maintained that "David Angel did *not* arrange the strings on my songs, he only did Bryan's . . . well, maybe he threw a couple of little things in there, but the trumpets and strings were all *my* ideas".

Arthur Lee, Bryan MacLean and Ken Forssi at Bido Lito's, fall '65

The *Da Capo* line-up of Love at the Bela Lugosi estate, 1966
L to R: Bryan MacLean, Ken Forssi, Snoopy Pfisterer, Michael Stuart,
Lee (top), Johnny Echols, Tjay Cantrelli

Love's Johnny Echols takes the mike, Bido Lito's

Luv 'n' Haight: a quintessential LA band comes to San Francisco

Bryan MacLean (left and above): "The most delectable prize in Hollywood"

Love, live and on record. Clockwise from top left: Cheetah, LA, 1968; Hollywood Bowl, 1966; first Elektra single, 1965, the *Four Sail* line-up (Lee in foreground; George Suranovich, left; Jay Donellan, top; Frank Fayad), late 1969

Love is back again. Four Sail on

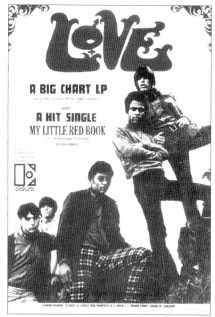

Alone again or: Lee post-*Changes*

Love *Out Here*: Lee, Frank Fayad, Gary Rowles, George Suranovich

Arthur in 1974; "There ain't nothin' that's going to stop me

"I'm a very private person"

Live and bewigged in the mid-90s

To John Tobler in May 1974, he claimed that working with Bruce Botnick on *Forever Changes* was "the worst experience" he'd ever had in the studio: "We were at each other's throats during the mixdown because we disagreed about the direction things should have gone . . . I can't figure out what he did except screw up the sound."

MacLean's Alone Again Or, the album's opening (and best-known) song, had been written for inclusion on Love's first album but wasn't completed properly till September '67, when it was still called Alone Again. (Lee added 'Or' perhaps just to make the title more interesting.) A brilliantly disingenuous ode to melancholy, the song was inspired by Bryan's memory of waiting for a girlfriend and based on Prokofiev's Lieutenant Kijé Suite. David Angel added a seven-piece string section, then wrote a Hispanic horn chart for a five-piece mariachi band that Botnick had used on a recent Tijuana Brass album.

> *Yeah, I heard a funny thing*
> *Somebody said to me*

That I could be in love with almost everyone
I think that people are the greatest fun
And I will be alone again tonight, my dear

"In a single self-contradictory lyric," wrote *Salon's* Sean Elder, "Love refuted the very, well, love that was flooding the airwaves. The other side of the transcendental experience was isolation – an isolation that felt all the more acute in the Summer of Love."

MacLean told me he "only became *interested* in the album when it came to the orchestration . . . I guess it was Botnick who picked out David Angel, who I think was doing arrangements for Andy Williams at the time". Bryan said that he himself "made reference to Rimsky-Korsakov and the Capriccio Espagnol. [David Angel] was one of the great orchestrators. And I said that if you could get the baroque-like strings of Haydn going under that trumpet . . . I didn't give David the actual notes. Those trumpet notes were his. But that was my contribution, blending those two concepts. And that was the happiest I ever was with anything we ever did as a band – the orchestral arrangement of that song."

He was a great deal less happy that Arthur Lee decided to remix the track and bring his own harmony vocal to the foreground of the song. When *Forever Changes* finally came out, the mix devastated him. "I listened to it once and never again," he says, incredible as that may sound. "I liked the original acetate: on Alone Again Or, my voice was stronger than Arthur's, but on the final mix, Arthur's harmony vocal is the main one you hear, so that sabotaged the melody."

"What you're actually hearing on the record isn't the melody," MacLean told David Fricke. "You hear Arthur's harmony, the third, sort of drony harmony. No one has actually heard how pretty that melody is. It's a much nicer melody than you think. But he did not have the confidence that my voice was strong enough to carry the song."

Curiously, *Forever Changes* fared considerably better in Britain than it did in America. Released in November 1967, as the year of the Summer of Love was drawing to a close, it reached Number 24 on the UK album chart. (In America it never rose any higher than Number 152.) By May 1968, moreover, Beat Instrumental magazine could report that "many people in the business" were already talking of the album as "a near-classic".*

In hindsight it could be argued that the British have been largely responsible for keeping the album's "classic" status alive over three decades, notwithstanding its reputation among neo-psychedelic acts in America. (A Zigzag poll in 1971 had *Forever Changes* as Best Album Ever, beating both *Sgt. Pepper* and *Blonde On Blonde*.) Among Love's most ardent admirers was Robert Plant, who gave Lee the red-carpet treatment after inviting him to a Led Zeppelin show at the Forum in LA in 1975. Since then, a host of British bands from The Teardrop Explodes to Teenage Fanclub has invoked the genius of Arthur Lee, while Alan McGee flew him over to London for Creation Records' 10th Anniversary bash at the Albert Hall. The indispensable Love fanzine, The Castle, is published by a schoolteacher in a small town in Cambridgeshire.

* The Rhino/Warners special edition of *Forever Changes* features Wonder People (I Do Wonder), the only unreleased song from the album's sessions, along with the instrumental Hummingbirds from the 7 And 7 Is session the previous year – prototype for The Good Humor Man. The single mix of Alone Again Or is different (though still not what Bryan was looking for), while the alternate mix of You Set The Scene features a vocal arrangement deleted from the album mix.

Masterpiece though it was, *Forever Changes* marked the beginning of the end for Love's original line-up. (The broken vase Lee is holding on the back cover of the original 1967 sleeve appears to be a statement about the band's disintegration – and perhaps also the end of flower power.) "I really wanted a Love band, a Love thing," Lee told me. "I wanted to be The Beatles, the Stones, a real unit, but everybody had different behaviour patterns. One guy was this way, another guy was that way, and I'm not Atlas, man, I can't hold up the world."

"As inconsistent as Arthur's been, he's much more together than anybody else when you think about the notorious people in that band," says Rhino's Harold Bronson. As Lee told John Tobler, "those guys couldn't cut it no more. I mean, like, they started doing weird things and I couldn't handle it. So I figured, you know, I ain't gonna stop, I'm gonna keep on rolling. I think it's right for me. No offence to anyone."

With Bryan wanting to go in a more soft-rock, ballad-oriented direction, Echols and Forssi tending more to the power-trio sound of Cream and Hendrix, and Arthur too stoned and disillusioned to pull them together, a split was almost inevitable. (International Times in London had already run a piece entitled "R.I.P. Love") There was one last release from Love Mk. 1, the amazing single Your Mind And We Belong Together b/w Laughing Stock, recorded at the end of January 1968. "They didn't do anything with it, and they always blamed me because I didn't travel," Lee told Tobler in December '74. On Laughing Stock, Lee directly addresses the band's unravelling. Indeed, it's possible that neither Bryan MacLean nor Johnny Echols were on the session. (Echols had possibly been arrested on drugs charges, which could mean that the wild guitar solo on Your Mind And We was played by Lee himself.)

"I was at the last Love sessions," David Anderle told Crawdaddy's Paul Williams. "We were cutting two more sides for what we thought at the time would be the next Love single. I was having my head blown sitting there, watching Love really getting it together, sounding better than they had ever sounded and being happier than I'd ever seen them in a recording studio."

Rhino/Warners' Special Edition of *Forever Changes* concludes with nine minutes of Love working on Your

Mind And We Belong Together in the studio – nine minutes which suggest Arthur Lee was as much a sonic visionary as the Brian Wilson of *Pet Sounds* and *Smile*. On the other hand, it took 44 takes for Arthur to get what he wanted on the track. As Ben Edmonds observes in his sleevenotes to the Special Edition, "the off-kilter grandeur of the finished product seems even more remarkable once we've glimpsed the process".

"You see how Arthur was in a kind of dictatorial position with the rest of the group and was interested in coaxing out of them the right performance," notes Andrew Sandoval, who helped to compile both *Love Story* and the *Forever Changes* Special Edition. "He really produced those sessions, especially on Laughing Stock and Your Mind; he had a very clear idea [of what he wanted]. With Your Mind, Arthur was actually in the control room while the band recorded the backing track. He later went in and overdubbed his acoustic guitar and vocals on top of that song. So he didn't cut that song live with the band. You can hear Arthur on the talkback after every take telling them what he wants. This doesn't sound like a band that's falling apart to me – it's a band that's pulled itself together after the shock of seeing session guys at the early stages of the *Forever Changes* production playing their music."

For some years rumours have swirled around that Your Mind and Laughing Stock were intended to be part of a fourth album by Love Mk. 1. But despite the existence of a working title, *Gethsemane*, this "lost" fourth album remains a mystery. Certainly Bryan MacLean knew nothing about it when I interviewed him in August 1996. And yet the Your Mind single was presaged in the UK by an advert from a shop called One Stop Records: "This track from the new Love LP – released in the States in mid-September – marks a change in direction back to the sound of their first LP."

One story has Jac Holzman rejecting the new material as "sub-standard Love" and returning the tapes to Arthur, who later burned them. According to The Castle fanzine, among the other songs for the album were three of MacLean's that fetched up on *ifyoubelievein* (Tired Of Sitting, People and Blues Singer), together with Lee's The Time Has Come For Some Counting To Be Done, Sixth Cents, Freeway Flyers, Peaceful Times Again and Uptown

'N Down, and finally the jointly-credited Sanctuary (Lee/Echols), and The Outlaw In Me (Lee/MacLean). According to Andrew Sandoval, all Lee will say of *Gethsemane* now is "Get-some-money"! "He will neither confirm, nor deny, its existence," Sandoval remarks. "And so too with Jac Holzman. So maybe – just possibly – it was Elektra that finished Love!"

MacLean was the first member of Love to jump ship.

"I went up to see Mike Gruber, who was managing the band at the time, and gave him my notice," he said. "Arthur was like, 'You can't quit, 'cos you're already fired!' Holzman and Anderle gave me a ticket for Hawaii and suggested I go off and write some songs. I think they were looking at the fact that at least two of the band members were irreparably hooked on heroin. Johnny was showing up without his guitar, trying to borrow guitars from other bands. I felt like I needed to get out while the getting was still good."*

The songs MacLean wrote – not in Hawaii but in

* MacLean himself has long been rumoured to have overdosed accidentally on heroin, despite not being a hardcore addict.

LA, where he stayed with his girlfriend Gail Parent (soon to be Frank Zappa's wife) – were subsequently recorded but turned down by Holzman, who told Zigzag in 1973 that Bryan had been to Elektra several times trying to get together a solo album, but hadn't convinced the label. "From what we could tell listening to tapes," Holzman later noted, "the best things he'd written were the old things like Orange Skies, Alone Again Or and Old Man."

"Jac said, 'Sorry, we're going to have to pass – everything's too fragmented,'" MacLean told David Fricke. "And in a way it was true. I wasn't ready to launch out on my own . . . I couldn't be a Tim Buckley. You have to remember, I had a low opinion of my singing, of my writing. I came from low self-esteem."

MacLean later went to New York to work on soundtracks for John G. Avildsen (of *Rocky* fame). After staying for three years, he signed to Capitol, then abandoned music and became a born-again Christian. The turning point, he explained, was sitting in a New York bar and feeling his drink "turn to sand" in his mouth. Bryan returned to live with his parents in Los Angeles, did various manual jobs and obtained a real estate licence.

But a Christian fellowship called the Vineyard was taking up increasing amounts of his time. He started singing at Friday night Bible classes, opened a Christian nightclub on Rodeo Drive called the Daisy, and served 10 years in the ministry.

And what of Arthur Lee? After Johny Echols, Ken Forssi and Michael Stuart quit Love, rumours began filtering through LA about the state the band's leader was in.

"I think Arthur got demoralised," said Bryan. "I think that happened to a lot of people in those days. We all thought we were on a rocket ship that was just going to continue to go straight up. I thought this was always going to be my life."

4 False Start

WHAT SAVED ARTHUR LEE WAS STROLLING into a Valley dive called the Brass Ring one night and seeing a band led by his old friend Noony Rickett.

Backed up by guitarist Gary Rowles, bassist Frank Fayad, and drummer George Suranovich – musicians Lee had himself occasionally played with in an early '60s band called The VIPs – Rickett was blasting out hard rock songs that fired Arthur up and made him question the music he'd been making with Love.

"They were playing You Got Me Floating and all kinds of things, and that drummer George . . . they really knocked me out," Lee recalled. After the show he told the band members they could make more money with him. Rickett soon found himself band-less.

"When I went out there, I had done this soft album and ... been influenced by what people told me to do," Lee told Lenny Kaye. "I'd even written my songs according to this trip of trying to get airplay and all this bullshit with the soft rock trip so that we could expand our group. And here this four-piece group was. They were as loud as fuck. They were out of sight. And, like, Jimi Hendrix had come out, and it really tripped me out that here's a cat who came out three years after I had seen The Byrds and freaked out and did his whole trip – he comes out and plays this loud music that I always wanted to do in the studio."

In addition to luring Fayad and Suranovich away from Rickett, Lee proceeded to hire lead guitarist Jay Donnellan (who before long would himself be replaced by Gary Rowles)*. In early 1969, the new Love set about

* Supposedly Donnellan's name wasn't actually Donnellan at all, it was Lewis. But Arthur decided Lewis wasn't groovy enough. After he'd fired him, Lee claimed that Jay had "freaked out": "It was the same trip, he was 21 years old, whatever, and it was the identical trip to my first group. He did the *Four Sail* album and got head-strong and he thought he had a little more weight than he had, I guess, and so he did a thing he shouldn't have done with his mouth and, you know, I had to get another guy."

recording almost 30 new songs, 10 of which made up *Four Sail*, a final album for Elektra in September 1969. The remainder were included on *Out Here*, Love's double-album debut for their new label Blue Thumb. All the tracks were cut in a vacant warehouse in LA on borrowed equipment.

When Suranovich couldn't make all the sessions, the curiously-named Drachen Theaker, formerly with Arthur Brown, played on five tracks. "It was like a soft rock band with a hard rock sound," Theaker recalled of the Love makeover. "Everything centred around Arthur's house, which was definitely psychedelic – on top of a mountain, with a swimming pool that was both inside and outside. We used to rehearse every day, but we only played gigs once or twice a month."

From the first bars of the opening August, the contrast between *Four Sail* and *Forever Changes* was immediate and striking. No strings or horns or even acoustic guitars in evidence this time; instead a busy, febrile four-piece sounding more like Cream than Love – at least until Lee's patent acid-Mathis vocal came in on the plangent first verse. Suranovich was all cross-cutting Ginger Baker rolls, while Donellan and Fayad sparred and widdled like a cut-price Clapton and Bruce.

The aforementioned Your Friend And Mine (Neil's Song) slowed things down. Drachen Theaker was on drums for this innocent-sounding Beatle-ish/Lovin' Spoonful-esque song about the overdose death of Neil Rappaport. "What about the time when you took my arm," sang Arthur in a breezily carefree style. "You said, 'Come with me, you don't have to be strong'/Said, 'Here's a little something to relax your mind/Now that we are two of a kind, my friend . . .'"

Among the other tracks on this perplexing and unconvincing record were the inoffensively jazzy Good Times and the nod to Eleanor Rigby that was Robert Montgomery, a song about the band's unofficial body-guard. Post-*Forever Changes*, noted Lee, "I started writing with the guitar rather than piano and the songs came out much funkier, and I've written like that ever since."

Elaborating later on the radical change in his writing style at this period, Lee said he'd "never realised that [*Forever Changes*] would create that much of a distur-bance . . . at the moment horns and strings don't seem to pop into my head like they once did. But sure, I'll do it again . . . I'm only a young man! It just seems far more important to other people that I do that than it does to me. Like someone saying, 'Hey man, you just invented the Hula Hoop, stick with it and you'll make a million dollars' . . . but that's not my bag. I did that, and you liked it – great. Now I'm doing this, check this out. 'But I don't like that, I think you should do this.' And I say to that: 'Look, if you like that, do it yourself! Ha ha!'"

Four Sail stiffed badly on both sides of the Atlantic. The double Out Here, released in the UK on the prog-rockish Harvest label only four months later in December 1969, reached Number 29 on the British chart. Despite stray echoes of the old Love on weak ballads like Doggone and Listen To My Song, the overriding impression gleaned from Out Here was that Lee the songwriter had lost his way, unsure whether he wanted Love to be Grand Funk Railroad (Stand Out) or Crosby, Stills & Nash (I Still Wonder).

A messy, sluggish electric version of the first album's chilling Signed D.C., with an overheated vocal by Arthur, only suggested regression. The sad truth is that virtually nothing Lee wrote after Your Mind And We Belong Together and Laughing Stock warrants comparison with even the most lightweight song on *Love*. Fayad and Suranovich may have been the best rhythm section he'd ever had, but the Lee of *Four Sail* and *Out Here* sounds bereft of genuine inspiration.

Even when Lee – finally touring the UK for the first time in early 1970 – joined forces with Jimi Hendrix in London and cut a bunch of glorified jam sessions at Olympic Studios, the tapes yielded nothing better than The Everlasting First, the indifferent first track on the execrable *False Start* (1970). If Lee felt that Hendrix had stolen his thunder as the original psychedelic soul dandy, he wasn't in Hendrix's league as a black rocker. It's no great surprise, really, that a mooted supergroup called Band-Aid, comprising Lee and Hendrix with Steve Winwood and Remi Kebaka from Traffic, never materialised.

Hendrix's impact on Lee cannot be underestimated, and had much to do with his change in musical direction. "Jimi was like Clark Kent to me," Arthur averred. "When he picked up the guitar he became Superman." Tellingly, Jac Holzman's son Adam remembered Lee taking him up to the Lookout Mountain house and playing *Are You Experienced?* "over and over again". "He kept getting up and saying, 'I'm going to have to listen to that one more time.' And he would put it back to Purple Haze."*

The point, surely, was that Lee, the prince of LA acid orch-pop, was finding it mighty hard to survive in the era of heavy electric rock. *Forever Changes* stood alongside *Sgt. Pepper*, but *Four Sail* and *Out Here* weren't fit to stand in the same room as *Electric Ladyland* or *Led Zeppelin II*. Occasional echoes of Love's great years – on Out Here's Gather Round, for example – weren't enough to redeem the wan material. It was hard to believe that the guy who was offering up I'll Pray For You and Keep On Shining was the same man who'd written 7 And 7 Is and The Red Telephone. But he was, and stranger things have happened in pop.

* Lee would always live in Hendrix's shadow, at once in awe of the man and envious of the greater impact he'd made. When a groupie approached him backstage at London's Rainbow Theatre in May 1974 and said, "You were great – Jimi Hendrix Number 2", Lee snapped back, "What's wrong with Arthur Lee Number 1?!" The girl told him Hendrix had been her favourite. "That's great," Arthur sneered. "Go dig him up!"

False Start was an unfortunate title for Love's second Blue Thumb release. The album certainly failed to live up to label boss Bob Krasnow's expectations.

"Blue Thumb was really funny," Lee told John Tobler. "Krasnow was boasting one day about how *False Start* was going to be in the Top 10 in the States, and I had a couple of my friends there. He's the president of the record company, strutting around like some rooster." When Krasnow said that if it didn't happen he'd let the group go, Lee promptly asked to have it in writing; Krasnow had little choice and obliged.

It should be pointed out that the post-*Forever Changes* Arthur Lee has his defenders, even champions. In a splendidly offbeat 1975 thinkpiece called "Good Day At Black Rock", Let It Rock writer Idris Walters described Lee as "a double-talking, instant-karma kid with his twists and turns, his puns and his treble negatives ... an Upsetter with an aura (deep maroon wine) to match Sri Chinmoy's", arguing that Lee's "continuing output shows progressive black consciousness as opposed to progressive rock consciousness."

For Walters, Arthur's early '70s music was all about

addressing his own blackness, in the same way that Hendrix moved into the black power era with *Band Of Gypsys*. Surmising that Lee was "having trouble with his white band and his white reputation" on *Four Sail* and *Out Here*, Walters pointed out that the lyrics to *False Start*'s The Everlasting First "tell the tale of black history rewritten ..."

Significantly, Lee referred several times to Miles Davis and drummer Tony Williams in his 1970 Jazz And Pop interview with Lenny Kaye. "My first drummer was a good back-beat drummer, you know," he said, "but now I want to do triplets and things and wherever I want to go with the people that I'm working with now . . . My drummer was influenced a lot by Tony Williams, so that's out of sight for me." Lee also talked about "getting funkier . . . a much funkier thing than anything we've done in the past.

"The thing about it now that I'm playing the rhythm guitar is that I can get more of the trip, more of the foundation that I wrote in the beginning, because I usually write with a guitar. And by me playing the licks instead of Bryan, where it was that way in the first three albums, I think I can get more out of myself by doing it myself."

More than anything, Lee stressed the urgency of hard work. "We've never done an all-out work campaign and that's what we've got to do," he conceded. "That's why we're in New York and that's why we went to London. We've got to plug the place with our trip if we want to be known . . .

"I'm planning on doing a lot better than I've ever done. No matter what your hobby is, or what you do in your personal life, you gotta keep the business thing together. Enough so that you can at least come back and do the same thing again. But I don't want to stop there. I'm planning on selling more records, and playing more places, than anything I've ever been involved in. And I know I'm gonna do it. There ain't nothing that's going to stop me. That's the way I feel. It's work time, and I'm ready to work."

Lee told Kaye he was going to find a new audience "by doing an appealing album. Working to get recognised all over again. A whole decade's gone by, 10 years. People who are 18 now were nine then . . . I don't know about nobody nine years old. But they're getting out in the world now, and they're aware of me, they know me. That's a good thing. For me not to be jumping on the wagon, making some bread, singing some good songs and doing some good music . . . I'd have to be out of my mind. I've always believed in making an honest living."

For all the gung-ho rhetoric, there was a long quiet period after the European dates of 1970. Lee virtually became a recluse, and the latest version of Love more or less disbanded. (Note that Johnny Echols and Ken Forssi were at this time incarcerated in San Luis Obispo Men's Colony for their doughnut-stand robberies.) But early in 1972 Alan MacDougall of A&M saw Arthur play a solo show at the Whisky A GoGo and got talking to him backstage about a deal.

Heavier and punchier than the hopeless albums by Love Mk. 2, the solo *Vindicator* (1972) was the result. (MacDougall described it as "hot and nasty boogie rock with flashes of pure beauty".) Two different sessions produced *Vindicator*, one featuring guitarist Charlie Karp, bassist David Hull and drummer Don Poncher – known collectively on the album as Band Aid, a nod to the mooted supergroup with Hendrix – the other featuring Poncher, guitarist Craig Tarwater, and Frank Fayad on bass.

"A guy who was a friend of mine by the name of Herbie Worthington introduced me to Charlie Karp and David Hull," said Arthur, "and Don Poncher, Craig Tarwater and Frank Fayad had been in Love . . . Herbie was running the house next door on the other estate I had . . ." (Tarwater, who'd been in the Sons Of Adam, was allegedly the inspiration behind Little Feat's Tripe Face Boogie.)

The guitarists kept things tight and gritty, and Lee's lyrics were pleasingly zany: song titles included You Can Save Up To 50% But You're Still A Long Ways From Home and Every Time I Look Up I'm Down, Or White Dog (I Don't Know What That Means). Love Jumped Through My Window, which almost sounds like *Man Who Sold The World*-era Bowie, was supposedly inspired by Lee's walking through the plate-glass door of his $80,000 house. Yet Everybody's Gotta Live was a lame John Lennon pastiche, and the power-trio-riffing You Want Change For Your

Re-Run showed that Lee was still struggling fruitlessly to emulate the deceased Hendrix.

For Idris Walters, *Vindicator* had "unique presence, a kind of black rock – not soul, not blues but Black Rock owing little to Chuck Berry . . . it is as though Lee were trying to harness the power of the essentially white rock guitar formula for the purposes of his emerging black political themes; as a means, perhaps, of resolving Sly's problem: 'Am I going to be jet-black or black as in a minstrel?'"

The album came out in August 1972, named after one of Arthur's dogs. On cover there were two Lees, a "Clean Sweep Janitor" holding out his hand expectantly for a tip from a berobed and bewigged rock star with guitar. To an extent the cover acknowledged the two sides of the Arthur Lee story: his underprivileged past, and his move into white rock world. (This was underlined, moreover, by the album's accreditation as "A Dr Hyde World-Wide Production".)

One of the album's themes was vegetarianism, exemplified by Hamburger Breath Stinkfinger and Ol' Morgue Mouth, both heavily influenced by repeated viewings of Fellini's Satyricon, which features countless animal carcasses. "I've seen the film 25 times or more, and I take people to see it," Lee remarked at the time. "I haven't eaten flesh since I first saw this movie, which was four years ago."

After *Vindicator* had been unfairly mauled by the critics, *Da Capo*/Doors producer Paul Rothchild approached Lee in July 1973 and offered to sign him to a new label called Buffalo, formed on a small budget by Rothchild and Michael Butler. Karp, Hull and Poncher were set to play on the album but left shortly before recording began; in their place came drummer Joe Blocker, guitarist Melvan Whittington and bassist Robert Rozelle. The latter pair had been part of Little Richard's road band.

The resulting *Black Beauty* never even made it to release. "Unfortunately the record company folded," Lee explained the following year. "They were under a guy [called] Michael Butler . . . he had the bread for the company, and the whole bit, and all of a sudden he changed his mind. So I had my album in the can there, and I couldn't get out of the contract 'til November, so that's one of the reasons I've been stagnant for the last couple of years."

May 1974 finally brought Lee and Love back to Europe, with a tour commencing at Bristol's Colston Hall and winding up with a date supporting Steely Dan in Amsterdam. The band was the *Black Beauty* line-up, augmented by guitarist John Sterling. "The whole thing is based around the people knowing I'm alive still, and I'm willing to work and do the whole bit," Lee told Zigzag's John Tobler. "Like, I footed the bill for this whole thing myself – I got four guys plus myself, and I'm paying for everything, so I just want everyone to know that I'm not after the fucking buck, or whatever you want to call it now. I like to play music and I've gone out of my way this time to do it . . ."

Lee resented having to play old crowd-pleasers like The Castle, and restricted himself oldies-wise to Alone Again Or, My Little Red Book and 7 and 7 Is. (He knew the *Black Beauty* musicians thought songs like Andmoreagain were uncool.) "I much prefer doing the things that I'm into now with my new group," he said, but added that he was "getting my old group together as soon as I get back from this tour . . . I don't know who exactly we'll be signing with, but we'll do an album and maybe some touring, and see what happens." Indeed, Bryan MacLean had been due to come to Europe with the band, "but the majority of the music we play is based around jazz and hard-rock type of things, and Bryan was more laid-back and acoustic . . ."

To some observers, Lee seemed bitter and unfulfilled on the 1974 tour. He toyed sadistically with interviewers, and rounded on the audience at the Rainbow Room atop London's ultra-hip Biba store. After casting a contemptuous glare at what Steve Samuels in Omaha Rainbow called "the mincing stewards and hair-tossing poseurs", Lee snapped, "You look so groovy out there, I could eat you all up . . . and spit you right out."

But Lee seemed happy when it was over. "The English concerts have been really good so far, so I'm gonna keep at it," he told Giovanni Dadomo. "I'm past 25 now so I figured it was time I did some hard work. I haven't had a hard life so far. Ha ha! But I figure if Chuck Berry can do it with no band, then I can do it with a little band-aid, ha ha!"

Lee said he was pleased by the loyalty of his latest

band: "My first group, man, we were making a whole lot of money and all that stuff, and these guys that I have now, man, haven't been making much money but they're still right there with me, and I'm with them . . ." And yet he remained paranoid about people deserting him: "I'm not confident, man, because this cat could walk out of this door right now, and I'd never see him again . . ." This seemed to be part of a more general unease: "I don't have confidence in anybody. You never know when they're going to croak."

After the Buffalo débâcle, Arthur was offered yet another one-album deal, this time by Robert Stigwood's RSO label, home most notably to Eric Clapton, whom Love supported on tour in the fall of 1974. The music press announced that Love had re-formed and would release an album called *Love, Together After All These Years*. But it wasn't true, and when the RSO album *Reel To Real* came out in January 1975 it was savaged even more mercilessly than *Vindicator*.

Produced by former Canned Heat manager Skip Taylor and featuring Joe Blocker on drums, Sherwood Akuna on bass, and Melvan Whittington and John

Sterling on guitars, *Reel To Real* was an attempt by Arthur to get back to his black soul roots – in Idris Walters' words "the last brush-off for the ageing hippies". Time Is Like A River (a tribute to incarcerated drummer/Hendrix sideman Buddy Miles) was *faux*-Al Green, while Stop The Music took its cue from Otis Redding's I've Been Loving You Too Long. A version of William De Vaughan's recent hit Be Thankful For What You Got underscored the message, even if the album was badly let down by insipid retreads of Busted Feet, Singing Cowboy and Everybody's Gotta Live.

"Right now, to me, Al Green is *all* right, *all* right, and of course Otis was definitely a trip, man," Lee told John Tobler. "I didn't dig Otis until he was dead, you know. At the time when I was wearing one shoe, I went to the Whisky and I saw Otis and his whole band was dressed in these little suits, all blue satin with white shirts and black ties, and, like, it was stupid on my part. I looked at the outside … I was sort of judging a book by its cover." He added that, "We've got a funk thing going in our group – it's good and black and everything, man, and that's just the way I feel."

Faux-soul it may have been, but Lee maintained his rock connections. An unlikely recipient of gratitude on *Reel To Real*'s sleeve was the one and only Keith Moon, who came to see Love at the Lyceum – sitting in a box in top hat and tails, no less. (Three years later, when Moon guest-hosted John Peel's Radio 1 show with the Bonzo Dog Band's Vivian Stanshall, he played *Vindicator*'s You Want Change For Your Re-Run.)

For Love's UK tour of May 1975 – the tour on which Moon saw the band – only John Sterling remained from the previous line-up. The bassist was Kim Kesterson, while on drums George Suranovich returned from the *Four Sail/Out Here* days. Lee was no less angry than he'd been the previous summer: at the Manchester Free Trade Hall show on May 6, he allegedly made racist comments and threatened to kick someone's teeth in. Stung by *Reel To Real*'s unsparing reviews and dismal sales, moreover, he was looking for someone to blame.

"To me, RSO didn't push *Reel To Real* too hard, but in the end the band got the blame," he told *NME*'s Max Bell during the tour. "See, the album didn't do shit in America and a lot of promises weren't kept. Publicity is the whole of the trip, and we ain't gettin' much. That gave me an excuse to get myself a new band, though – 'cos you always gotta try better things. I'm not saying this band are any better than the others and whaddya mean by the word 'better' anyway? I like the way both bands play. I can groove with that. It's cool with me, man."

Defending his decision to strive for a blacker sound, Lee told Bell: "All my music should have had a black sound. I've [had a black feel] since I started. I been black all the time, heh heh." He said he'd listened to black music all his life. "I listen to the radio and the black stations may have influenced me, so what's wrong with that groove? See, in 1965 I started what I did, that style of shit."

Asked about re-forming the original Love, he said he thought it was a bad idea: "Seems kinda corny to me. Kenny Forssi didn't want to do it 'cos he expects a percentage. I don't see how these cats can deserve that after all this time when I kept the trip going. I don't mind sharing the gig, but to get a piece of the cake, man, you should earn it. Just to come back in the groove because you been there before, that's an entirely different ball game." Yet he conceded that he was writing songs in the *Forever Changes* vein again: "Must have been brainwashed by so many people talking about that like it was the best album I made, you dig?"

Arthur's general edginess and belligerence in this period had more than a little to do with his drug intake. Robert Rozelle claimed he watched Lee shoot quantities of cocaine that "would have killed a normal person. He had a constitution like a horse." Rozelle himself was on the receiving end of Lee's rage on more than a few occasions: once, after Rozelle had demanded the repayment of a loan he'd made to him, Lee chased him out of the house with a gun. When Rozelle jumped into his car, Lee "pointed the gun at the windshield, so I ducked and put the car in drive and drove off the hillside". Rozelle ended up in a neighbour's backyard.

"Melvan Whittington said that when Arthur saw me go over, he just turned around and walked in the house and started sweeping the kitchen," Rozelle later laughed. "He said, 'Well, he's dead, so I might as well start cleanin' up before they come get me.'"

When Lee realised Rozelle was still alive, he came racing down the hillside: "He grabbed me, hugged me, kissed me on the cheek, and carried me back up the hill. He said, 'Man, why'd you do that to me? Man, I love you.'

"Why'd *I* do that to *him*? The boy was nuts."

5 Forever Changes

BY 1976, LEE HAD ALL BUT QUIT THE MUSIC business and was working with his stepfather house-painting in south-central LA. "When I left the band," Bryan MacLean told me in 1996, "nothing ever happened for Arthur again, and I think that just galls him. He's probably more bitter and resentful over that than anything."

MacLean glossed over the fact that nothing much had happened for him either, although he did write Don't Toss Us Away for the 1985 debut album by his half-sister Maria McKee's band Lone Justice – and later had the song covered by country songbird Patty Loveless.

The mid-'70s had seen MacLean bottoming out on

booze and turning to Christianity in an attempt to halt the unravelling of his life. He later worked as janitor at the Pico Drug store in West LA and at Pep Boys Autoparts in the Crenshaw district, all the while regularly attending a Baptist church.

One person who knew MacLean at this point in his life was Love fanatic Robert Leslie Dean, who in the next decade would be a member of The Bryan MacLean Band. "My brother and I tried to get in touch with Arthur to see if maybe we could help him out or get him a contract or something," Dean recalls. "We met him and tried to help him, but we got burned and got scared. At that time we also found out – in a roundabout way – how to get to Bryan. This was in August of 1976, 10 years after 7 And 7 Is, and we met with Bryan at Cafe Figaro in West Hollywood."

Bryan told the Dean brothers that he was the music director of the Vineyard, a church fellowship out in the Valley, and invited them to come see him perform there. "He blew us away with the quality of his voice and his folk guitar picking," Dean says. "He still sounded like the guy who sang Old Man and Softly To Me, only he was doing spiritual Christian music – melodic, open-chorded, folky."

In 1978, John Sterling encouraged Arthur Lee to re-form the original Love. No full reunion took place, but – surprisingly – MacLean came on board, and the line-up was completed by Kim Kesterson (bassist on the 1975 tour) and Knack drummer Bruce Gary. Commemorated by a live album recorded at the Whisky on October 20, these shows were far from happy occasions.

"It was another case of Arthur spinning out and me going, 'OK, I've already experienced this, I'll see you around,'" MacLean remembered. "It's like the blush of youth goes and then it's just sort of the bitterness that starts to surface, and the anger, and the resentment. He's one of those people who'd like to go back to the times when everything was just so sweet and fresh and new."

By the early '80s, MacLean was playing shows with Maria McKee, duetting with her on Orange Skies and Alone Again Or (and even demo'ing a version of No. 14). The rest of the band comprised Robert Leslie Dean (vocals, rhythm guitar, keyboards), an 18-year-old half-black/half-Egyptian bassist, and Little Richard veteran

Charles Connor on drums – not exactly a rhythm section suited to Bryan's style.

Lee, meanwhile, was offered yet another one-album deal, this time by Jeff Gruber's E.X.Pressions. The concept was to recreate the style of *Forever Changes* on an album provisionally entitled *More Changes* – except using synths rather than real strings. In the end, the album was never released, though certain tracks (including a version of Jimmy Cliff's Many Rivers To Cross) later saw the light of day.

Another *Best Of Love* appeared in 1980 on Rhino, the LA reissue label which also released the very sub-par 1981 album *Arthur Lee*, featuring a new version of 7 And 7 Is. *Studio/Live* (MCA, 1982) was a perplexing release, the studio album comprising nothing more than an assort-ment of tracks from *Out Here* and the live half purporting to be from a Fillmore East show in December 1970 (disputed by Lee, who claimed the recordings were from the Boston Tea Party in the same month).

Lee played on the same bill as Bryan MacLean one night at the Whisky in March 1982. Drunk, Arthur is said to have made disparaging remarks during Bryan's set, and even to have thrown a cup of coffee over him. (Significantly, perhaps, Bryan performed three of the songs which had been rejected during the *Forever Changes* sessions: People, Tired Of Sitting and Blues Singer.)

Following *Arthur Lee*, the man all but disappeared for the best part of a decade – ostensibly to help look after his stepfather Clinton, who was dying of cancer, but also because of fatigue and disillusionment. "I was tired of signing autographs," Lee told Phil Gallo. "I was tired of being BS'd out of my money. I got tired of the Hollywood set. I got tired of hearing every new group remind me of a song I had written. I just got tired."

Lee's health wasn't improving, either. Bruce Botnick recalled a night in the late '80s when he was walking along Sunset. "This bum stopped me, scared the hell out of me," he told Sara Scribner. "He said, 'Hey man, do you have any money?' He was obviously strung out. It was Arthur, and he didn't even recognise me." (Lee denied this: "I've had hard times, but I've never been a beggar . . .")

"It was difficult to reconcile in my mind that the writer who just wrote really amazing, articulate, literate lyrics was the same person sitting across from you, talking to you," Rhino's Harold Bronson recalled. "If you look at Arthur and what he's done musically and how literate and inspired his lyrics are, despite how he comes across, you have to think that inside there's an intelligent person. Someone who's less smart could not have done what he's done. But from time to time I've just heard of him doing the stupidest things."

With his profile raised by The Damned's 1987 cover of Alone Again Or, Lee played at the Psychedelic Summer Of Love in LA's Universal Amphitheater on January 27, 1989. Yet he was becoming more unpredictable, even schizoid, on-stage, often shouting at his backing bands during shows, and constantly sacking managers.

A new manager, Mark Linn, got Lee back on track, playing decent shows with a revived Love made up of long-lost Don Conka (drums), former Zappa sideman (and son of R&B legend Johnny) Shuggie Otis (guitar), Sherwood Akuna (bass) and the ever-trusty Melvan Whittington (guitar). Whittington also played on *Arthur Lee And Love*, a new album for the French label New Rose that boasted Five String Serenade, Lee's best song in years. "That New Rose album was really good," said Greg Shaw.

"It's amazing that he pulled that together from the garbage of his life and cocaine addiction and a completely twisted mind."

With Linn motivating him, Lee experienced a sense of rejuvenation. In May 1992 he went to Europe to play a handful of dates in Paris, London and Liverpool. Backing him were a band called Shack, led by two brothers who'd been awestruck Love disciples since they were teenagers.

"As soon as we heard the first Love album, it was just like, This is it, this is special," says John Head, younger sibling and Shack's lead guitarist. "There was something in it that was just different for us. We got into them from that moment. It was the honesty of the music, the fact that it wasn't contrived. And maybe the mystique about the band as well, the fact that they didn't move out of LA and they lived in Bela Lugosi's house. For me when I was fuckin' 13, it was just like, Wow, come on. But first and foremost it's just the fuckin' music – it's special, and no-one's really heard of them. It was like, Wow, look at this secret, this pot of gold we've found!"

Head points out that Liverpool bands have always

loved Love. "When the Bunnymen and the Teardrops were working at Zoo, they were into Love and I think very influenced by them," he says. His older brother Michael would cover She Comes In Colors with his first band The Pale Fountains, and his songwriting has drawn from Love's well ever since. Head's solo *The Magical World Of The Strands* is possibly the best Love album since *Forever Changes*, while Shack's *HMS Fable* is the missing link between Arthur Lee and Lee Mavers . . . or Sunset Strip and Merseyside.

The brothers, says John, were "flabberghasted" when their French friend Stéphane Bismuth informed them he'd just been to see Arthur in Los Angeles; even more so when he asked if they'd be prepared to back the man on two UK dates. Nor was Lee a disappointment when they finally got to meet their hero in Paris.

"He was just a really sound guy," says Head. "We just got on immediately, and he respected us for what we were doing and he could sense the respect we had for him. He knew how much we loved him 'cos we fuckin' told him. He was a well-honest, genuine guy, and as cool as you can fuckin' get! He's also a very alert person, he can suss the room out without lifting his head from a cup of tea. He's well together on that score."

For Head, the Paris show was magical: "Everyone was just standing open-mouthed in awe of this guy. No-one took their eyes off him, including us – it was the first time we'd seen him. When everyone was shouting for an encore, we just pushed him out on his own. He wanted us to go back on, but we said, No, man, they're here to see you. And we ran round the front and watched him from the audience."

The Liverpool show, at the Academy, was even more of a mind-blower. "It was just a ridiculously weird thing to be doing," laughs Head. "To be backing Arthur Lee in my own home town was like winning the lottery. When he saw this room full of people of all ages singing his songs, it really moved him. And you could see how much it meant to him. You had guys with grey beards and you had 14-year-old girls and lads. The day after the show, I saw a girl about 14 walking around with a LOVE T-shirt on."

Summer 2000 saw the belated release of the bootleg-quality *Arthur Lee Live In Liverpool 1992*, a souvenir of the Academy show put out by Mike Badger and Paul Hemmings of Viper Records. "I thought it was terrible, because Arthur's in prison and not getting any help from the bootlegs," said Badger. "Arthur's attorney said Arthur would appreciate any help we could give him." *Live In Liverpool* featured a smattering of classics from the first three Love albums and three more recent songs: the paranoid Somebody's Watching You, Passing By (effectively a tribute to Muddy Waters), and a version of Everybody's Gotta Live that incorporated a verse from John Lennon's Instant Karma.

"When the concert started, I was glad to see both young and old enjoying the show," Lee wrote to MOJO on the album's release. "When I wrote *Forever Changes*, I didn't think about a time period, only about what I saw happening around me, and it seems those things still are. The show in Liverpool is still the most memorable of my life. It did not stop at the concert either: when I left the club they followed me!! I slipped into a restaurant, and thought I had lost them and began to relax. The people in the restaurant then began to sing what I thought was for someone's birthday, but as I listened the songs became familiar. I could not believe it!! It blew me away!! I would like to thank the people of Liverpool for their warmth and their love."

Back in America, Lee began playing a lot more regularly. In Los Angeles he was backed by a young quartet called Baby Lemonade, made up of Mike Randle (lead guitar), Rusty Squeezebox (guitar), Henry Liu (bass) and David Green (drums). (Randall and Squeezebox were, like Arthur, light-skinned blacks, and Liu was Chinese-American.) "We opened for him at the Troubadour," Squeezebox told Steve Powell. "He loved our music, fired his band on the spot, and asked us to be Love."

On June 20, 1993, I saw Lee with Baby Lemonade at the Palomino, a run-down roots-rock dive in the San Fernando Valley. The band were still feeling their way around the material, and seemed oddly insensitive to the delicacy of songs like Orange Skies and Signed D.C. Lee himself weathered the constant calls for his famous songs, though he claimed he was "so nervous I don't know what to do with myself". Still strikingly handsome in black jeans and Cuban heels – though still sporting a desperately unconvincing hairpiece – he eventually relaxed enough to enjoy himself on A House Is Not A Motel and 7 And 7 Is. Love's next gig would be a support to Doors tribute band Wild Child, and if you don't think *that's* ironic, paint me black.

"We had to prove ourselves to the sceptics, and we felt a big weight," said Mike Randle. "But as time went by, we felt more and more comfortable. The only problems were when we'd have Love shows and Arthur would forget to tell us!" The group even recorded new versions of 7 And 7 Is, Feathered Fish and Your Mind And We Belong Together with Lee in Chicago.

Arthur could still be testy. At a July 1994 show in San Juan Capistrano to promote the Love tribute album *We're All Normal And We Want Our Freedom*, he was so abusive to Baby Lemonade during the set that they resigned after the gig. Somehow things were patched up later.

That summer he was back in London, appearing at the Creation birthday party celebrations and playing a gig at the Garage in Islington with the acclaimed High Llamas as his backing band. (The 1998 *Oncemoreagain* bootleg features 12 tracks from the show.)

Another band who backed Lee as "Love" were Das

Damen, who played a number of shows with him on the East Coast. "He's way out there but also pretty sharp and his voice is still incredible," recalled Alan Licht. "His current material is a joke, but he's basically a downhome guy, a sweet guy."

In 1995, with Rhino's sumptuously-packaged 2-CD *Love Story* about to come out, everything started to go badly wrong again. In the early summer, Lee and his white girlfriend Susan Levine were at a supermarket near their Sherman Oaks apartment when someone made a racist remark and Lee supposedly pulled a gun. "There was no gun," Levine told Sara Scribner. "There wasn't even a water pistol. We just left. I don't understand how that even got into court. It was absurd."

On June 29, the LAPD came to the couple's apartment on Kester Avenue after her parents heard what sounded like a fight on the end of the phone. Levine appeared to have been beaten up but said she'd hit her head on a coffee table. The police decided it was spousal battery and pressed charges.

Bailed out by Rhino, Lee got his act together for a promotional tour with Baby Lemonade. "Arthur had too much to drink the first night of our tour, but he never got like that again," said Mike Randle. "He was healthy for the whole tour and didn't mess with anything. And as a matter of fact, people were trying to give it to him, and he was saying no. He didn't have any babysitters there. He could've done anything he wanted to."

But Arthur was already in much deeper shit. On June 10, police had been called to the Kester Avenue apartment by a neighbour who claimed that Lee had fired a shot, then pointed a gun at him and threatened to "blow him away".

"It was total rubbish," says Doug Thomas, who not only was with Arthur that Saturday night in July 1995 but claims the gun in question was fired, accidentally, by himself. A drummer who'd played for 30 years in West Coast-influenced bands in his native New Zealand, Thomas was visiting Lee in LA to discuss the possibility of releasing some new Love songs. "We were planning to put out an album called *Forever Changes II*," he told me. "Arthur has a whole bunch of great songs no-one's ever heard."

Thomas said that he and his wife were sitting around with Lee and Levine, drinking wine and watching a video of the Steve Martin comedy Three Amigos. At some point, Lee asked Thomas to look through some old boxes for videos of recent Love shows in Europe. Upon opening one such box in a closet belonging to Lee's ex-girlfriend, Thomas found what turned out to be a Magnum .44.

"I'd never seen a handgun before, and I wasn't even sure if it was a real one," he said. "So I pulled it out, walked through to the patio and said, Hey, Arthur! *Arriba!* The second time I pulled the trigger it went off, making the biggest noise I've ever heard."

Lee and Levine immediately grabbed the gun, since both knew that – as a felon who'd been convicted on a couple of assault and drugs charges in the '80s – Lee could land in serious trouble for possessing such a thing. Thomas maintained that Arthur had no idea the gun was in his ex-girlfriend's closet – that it had been sent to the apartment by his new manager George, who'd thought the box contained a computer. "George was lending Arthur his computer so he could start selling his albums on the net, but Arthur hadn't got around to opening the box."

After a short while, about 10 policemen arrived, handcuffed Lee and the others, and took Lee to the Van Nuys central police station. A few hours later, they searched the apartment in Sherman Oaks and found a box of 500 armour-piercing bullets (also received unknowingly from Lee's manager, according to Doug Thomas). This immediately placed Lee in the categories of suspected terrorist and suspected police killer. They also found a small amount of a Class A drug in his ex-girlfriend's handbag. All in all, there were seven charges brought against him before he was released on bail.

When Lee left LA to tour Europe in the summer, various fans suggested he stay in France or Spain as an exile rather than risk imprisonment by returning home. "He said he wouldn't," says Doug Thomas. "He said he was going back to prove his innocence." Little did Lee know that when the case came to trial he would be up against a notorious DA known as "The Dragon Woman" and a jury bussed in – like the jury which acquitted the LAPD officers in the Rodney King case – from Simi Valley.

"I felt like the judge let the prosecution get away with murder," Lee told Sara Scribner from prison. "And, as far as the jury was concerned, I might as well have been Rodney King in Simi Valley . . . I felt like I was in hell or, what's worse, somewhere where I wasn't going to get a fair trial, and I didn't."

"Out of the 12 jurors, there were nine middle-class whites and three Asians," says Thomas. "There were no black people on the jury, and the Asians had just moved to America, so they didn't want to rock the boat and agreed with whatever the white jurors said. I think the judge was fair, but the DA was out to get Arthur and she totally twisted the jury's minds with her account. My particular account took three half-days. They actually stopped the proceedings and asked if I realised I could be charged with perjury. I said I did, but I couldn't have another man going to jail for something bloody stupid that I did."

The jury ignored Thomas's evidence and found Lee guilty on all charges. With enhancements attached to the charge because of his prior felony conviction and the other events of that month, the court threw the book at him: 12 years, 85 per cent of time served: nine-plus years in prison. He was taken to LA County Jail, where he awaited transfer to State Prison.

"I think that Arthur had an incredibly unfair trial, it's almost not accurate to describe it as a trial," his lawyer William Genegos said. "What happened was he was not willing to admit that he did it, and he wanted to go to trial, and people who go to trial get punished for it."

"I have no idea how a judge could say the abusive things he said to Arthur," said Mike Randle. "She said he was a danger to society. Said he'd done things like driving without insurance since 1963. Name me one other rock star that hasn't. Robert Downey Jr has four felony counts. Arthur's only got three. It was a complete scam, a complete travesty. It says a lot about America, its obsession with sending people to jail and its complete and utter disrespect for its artists." *They're locking them up today, and throwing away the key . . .*

In April 1997, Randle helped to stage A Love Affair, a benefit gig at the Ash Grove designed to raise funds for Lee's defence and awareness of his plight. The show was "sparsely attended". Among the performers were original Love drummer Don Conka, Don's daughter's band Fish N' Chips, and longtime back-up group Baby Lemonade.

Lee's case infuriated fans such as the Bevis Frond's Nick Saloman, who gave an irate speech about Lee's plight when his band played the Silver Lake club Spaceland in 1996. "I think the draconian kind of sentence he received is appalling," Saloman says now. "I think it's an absolute travesty that someone like that's shut away. We should be erecting statues for him, not locking him away in prison."

Lee had been in prison for over a year when his old Love partner (and rival) Bryan MacLean was rushed to Cedars-Sinai Medical Center after a massive heart attack on Christmas Day, 1998. Fifty-two years old, he was dead on arrival in the late afternoon.

"He never married, never had children," says his friend Robert Leslie Dean. "But one of the last things Bryan told me before he passed was, 'This is the last year I go without having a wife.' I think there was quite a strain on Bryan to want to get into a relationship with a loving woman. The official cause of death was a heart attack, but I also see a broken heart there."

MacLean, sometime pop heartthrob of Sunset

Strip, had released *ifyoubelievein* the year before. "I think I might finally be starting to grow up," he'd told sleevenote writer David Fricke. "To be a responsible person, someone who's not going to spin out."

Epilogue
Andmoreagain

*The wreck of the Arthur Lee/Will never return
again/Never return again.*

Robyn Hitchcock & The Egyptians, 1993

ARTHUR SINKS THE DREGS OF ANOTHER
Bloody Mary and fixes me with a leery glare.

"I don't know anything about acid at all," he almost
snaps. "I'm not a Timothy Leary follower. I have nothing
good to say about any drugs or alcohol for young people.
I'm not going to elaborate on anything that would put a
dent in a young person's mind. I've been out there, man. Now
I just live in an apartment, don't worry about the butcher."

Drunk and mumbling, Arthur is starting to get crabby. My interview, in the summer of 1993, is winding up.

Eight years on, Arthur Lee's influence is still everywhere in pop culture. Bands from The Ramones to Yo La Tengo have been profoundly affected by him. "Look at his body of work," says Bruce Botnick, now a successful soundtrack producer. "It's had a big impact. I turn on the radio, I know what they're listening to."

One can hear Love not only in Shack's dark, haunting Daniella but in Badly Drawn Boy's Stone On The Water and Superstar's worshipful I Love Love. Contemporary movies feature Love songs: I Shot Andy Warhol has Gimi A Little Break, Hideous Kinky Alone Again Or.

Lee, meanwhile, languishes in Pleasant Valley State Prison in central California, spending his days exercising and reading the Bible.

"This has been so humiliating to me, being convicted of something I did not do. I didn't think it would go this far, so I didn't want to broadcast it. Now I have another chance."

He has twice appealed against his conviction and twice lost.

Lee still cares enough about his legend to help keep the Love flame alive. "When they stop talking about you, that's when you're in trouble," he told Sara Scribner, his mordant sense of humour clearly intact. "That's why I've got to get out of here. I've got to start stirrin' up more stories."

Let's go back to the original question: is Arthur Lee a genius or a rogue? Or is he both, half intimidating hood, half sweet-natured Pied Piper? More than a few of his acquaintances have suggested he is nothing less than a borderline schizophrenic. "Arthur is not of this world," Jac Holzman once remarked. "He lives in a world of his own creation."

"It's hard to say how deep the imbalance and lack of integrity go with Arthur," said the born-again Bryan MacLean, somewhat sternly. "He lacked repentance, *always.*"

"People always sort of look on Arthur as a failure or a negative," Shack's John Head counters. "And I'd just like to say he's not a negative. He's definitely a positive."

At the end of my 1993 interview with Lee, the tipsy smile left his face for a second and he looked me hard in the face. "I'm a very private person," he said. "Chico Hamilton said the music is in the street, but for me, the music is in *me*. I *am* the music."

Timeline

MARCH 7, 1945 Arthur Lee born Arthur Porter Taylor, Memphis, TN.

APRIL 1965 Pre-Love group The Grass Roots make their live debut in LA.

SUMMER 1965 Bryan MacLean joins the group; The Grass Roots will subsequently rename themselves Love to avoid confusion with a similarly named act.

JANUARY 24, 1966 Love record their self-titled debut album at Sunset Sound Studio.

MAY 1966 *Love* makes US 57.

JUNE 1966 A cover of Bacharach/David's My Little Red Book makes US 52.

SEPTEMBER 1966 *7 And 7 Is* makes US 33.

SEPTEMBER 27, 1966 Group begins work on second album, *Da Capo*, at RCA-Victor studio.

MARCH 1967 *Da Capo* makes US 80.

JUNE 9, 1967 Lee begins recording *Forever Changes* with LA session crew due to friction within the group. Band members are shocked at the thought of being left off their own album, and Love resolve to settle their differences.

AUGUST 11, 1967 Love reconvene for further sessions at Sunset Sound – without any session players present. Album, with orchestral overdubs, completed by later September.

NOVEMBER 1967 *Forever Changes* peaks at UK 24 and US 152.

JANUARY 1968 Alone Again Or reaches US 99. Soon after, Bryan MacLean leaves the group.

SEPTEMBER 1969 Lee, with new version of Love, released *Four Sail*, the band's last album for Elektra. It reaches US 102.

MAY 1970 *Out Here*, including material from *Four Sail* sessions, hits released on the Blue Thumb label UK 29 and US 176.

DECEMBER 1970 *False Start* released, featuring yet another line-up.

AUGUST 1972 Lee, now a solo artist, signs to A&M and releases the poorly received *Vindicator*.

1973 *Love Masters* compilation released.

DECEMBER 1974 Lee re-emerges with new line-up of Love. They sign to RSO and issue *Reel To Real*.

1977 Reunion with Bryan MacLean comes to nothing, though the two will join forces two years later for some dates in California.

JANUARY 27, 1989 Arthur & Love perform in LA at the Psychedelic Summer Of Love festival. French label New Rose released an album of new material, titled *Arthur Lee And Love*.

MAY 1992 Lee embarks on European tour, backed by Liverpool
    band Shack. He begins gigging regularly.

JUNE 1994 Lee performs at Undrugged, Creation Records' 10th
    anniversary party at London's Royal Albert Hall and at the
    Garage in Islington.

JUNE 10, 1995 Police are called to Lee's LA apartment after
    neighbour claims the singer had threatened him with a
    gun. Lee is subsequently jailed for 12 years.

DECEMBER 25, 1998 Bryan MacLean dies after a massive heart
    attack, aged 52.

Discography

My Little Red Book/Message To Pretty (EK 45603, March 1966, US)

My Little Red Book/Hey Joe (HLZ 10073, June 1966, UK)

7 & 7 Is/No. 14 (HLZ 10073, September 1966, UK)

7 & 7 Is/No. 14 (EK 45605, 1967, US)

She Comes In Colors/Orange Skies (EKSN, 1967, UK)

Stephanie Knows Who/Orange Skies (EK 45608, 1967, US)

She Comes In Colors/Orange Skies (EK 45608, 1967, US)

Softly To Me/The Castle (EKSN 45016, 1967, UK)

Que Vida/Hey Joe (EK 45613, March 1967, US)

Alone Again Or/Bummer In The Summer (EKSN 45024, 1967, UK)

The Daily Planet/Andmoreagain (EKSN 45026, 1967, UK)

Alone Again Or/A House Is Not A Motel (EK 45629, January 1968, US)

Your Mind And We/Laughing Stock (EKSN 45038, September 1968, UK)

I'm With You/Robert Montgomery (EKSN 45068, 1969, UK)

Alone Again Or/Good Times (EK 45700, August 1970, US)

Alone Again Or/Bummer In The Summer (EK21010, October 1970, UK)

Alone Again Or/My Little Red Book (Spun Gold EK 45056, 1970, US/UK)

Stand Out/Doggone (HAR 5014, March 1970, UK)

I'll Pray For You/Stand Out (BLU 106, May 1970, US)

The Everlasting First/Keep On Shining (HAR 5030, October 1970, UK)

Keep On Shining/The Everlasting First (BLU 116, November 1970, US)

Keep On Shining/Flying/Ride That Vibration/Love Is Coming (Stateside 016–92401, 1970, US)

Everybody's Gotta Live/Love Jumped Through My Window (A&M 1361, August 1972, US, released as a Arthur Lee solo single)

Sad Song/You Want Change For You Re-Run (A&M 1381, November 1972, US, released as an Arthur Lee solo single)

Alone Again Or/Andmoreagain (EK 12113, July 1973, UK)

Alone Again Or/The Castle (Treasured Tracks, September 1973, UK)

Time Is Like A River/With A Little Energy (RSO 502,

December 1974)

Time Is Like A River/You Said You Would (RSO 2090 151, 1974, UK)

You Said You Would/Good Old Fashioned Dream (RSO 506, March 1975, US)

I Do Wonder/Just Us/Do You Know The Secret/Happy You (CAP 1001, 1977, UK, released as the *Da Capo EP*)

Alone Again Or/Andmoreagain (E 9740, April 1984, UK)

Girl On Fire/Midnight Sun (DR 1017, 1994, US)

VINYL LPs

Love (EKS 74001, September 1966)

Da Capo (EKS 74005, February 1967)

Forever Changes (EKS 74013, February 1968)

Four Sail (EKS 74049, November 1969)

Out Here (BTS 9000/SHDW 3/4, March 1970)

Love Revisited (EKS 74058/Z 469009, December 1970)

False Start (BTS 8822/SHVL 787, January 1971)

Vindicator (A&M SP 43561, August 1972, released as an Arthur Lee solo album)

Love Masters (K 32002, February 1973)

Reel To Real (RSO 4804/RSO 239415, January 1975)

Best Of Love (RNLP 800, 1980)

Arthur Lee (RNLP 020/BEGA 26, July 1981, released as an Arthur Lee solo album)

Love Live: 1978 Reunion (RNDF 251, 1982, picture disc)

Love Live (Line 625047/5153, 1982, German release)

Studio/Live (MCA 27025, 1982)

Golden Archive – Best of Love (RNLP 70175, 1986)

Out There (Big Beat Wika 69, July 1988)

Arthur Lee & Love (New Rose Rose 288, May 1992, French release)

IFYOUBELIEVEIN (Sundazed LP 5056, 1996, released as a Bryan
    MacLean solo album)

Forever Changes (Warners reissue, 180g vinyl, 755960659-1, 2000)

*Shack Accompany Arthur Lee: A Live Performance At The Academy,
    Liverpool, May 1992* (Viper LP 003, 2000)

Love (Sundazed LP 5100, 180g vinyl, 2001)

Da Capo (Sundazed LP 5101, 180g vinyl, 2001)

Forever Changes (Sundazed LP 5102, 180g vinyl, 2001)

Four Sail (Sundazed LP 5103, 180g vinyl, 2001)

Love Re-Visited (Sundazed LP 5104, 2001)

CD RELEASES

Four Sail (Thunderbolt CDBT 047, July 1986, UK)

Forever Changes (Elektra 74013-2/WEA 9606 562, 1987, US/UK)

Love (Elektra 74001-2, 1988, US)

Da Capo (Elektra 74005-2, 1988, US)

False Start (One Way/MCAD 22029, 1990, US)

Out Here (One Way/MCAD 22030, 1990, US)

Out There (Big Beat CDWIK 69, 1990, UK)

Studio/Live (One Way/MCAD 22036, 1991, US)

False Start (BGO CD 127, 1991, UK)

Arthur Lee & Love (New Rose Rose CD288, May 1992, French release)

Five String Serenade (New CD166, 1992, French release)

Love Comes In Colors (RV CD29, 1992, Australian compilation release)

Love Story (Elektra/Rhino Traditions R 273500, compilation 2-disc box set, US)

Vindicator (A&M Remasterpieces 540 697–2 540 697–2, 1997, reissue with extra tracks)

IFYOUBELIEVEIN (Sundazed SC 11051, 1997, US, released as a Bryan McLean solo album)

Shack Accompany Arthur Lee: A Live Performance At The Academy, Liverpool, May 1992 (Viper CD 003, 2000, UK)

Candy's Waltz (Sundazed 11076, 2000, US, released as a Bryan McLean solo album)

Forever Changes (Elektra Traditions/Rhino 8122–73537–2, 2001, reissue with extra tracks)

Love Live In Concert: Electrically Speaking (Yeaah 49, 2001, UK)

Note: *Love*, *Da Capo*, *Forever Changes* and *Vindicator* were also made available in Japan, the releases included booklets of lyrics. There is a video available, *Arthur Lee & Love* (Iceworld Outlaw 99, 1991)